W9-CCY-326

Teach Yourself
VISUALLY™
Photoshop® CS4

Visual

by Mike Wooldridge and

Linda Wooldridge

WILEY

Wiley Publishing, Inc.

Teach Yourself VISUALLY™ Photoshop® CS4

Published by
Wiley Publishing, Inc.
10475 Crosspoint Boulevard
Indianapolis, IN 46256

www.wiley.com

Published simultaneously in Canada

Library of Congress Control Number: 2008939709

ISBN: 978-0-470-33947-3

Manufactured in the United States of America

10 9 8 7 6 5 4 3 2 1

Trademark Acknowledgments

Contact Us

For general information on our other products and services please contact our Customer Care Department within the U.S. at 800-762-2974, outside the U.S. at 317-572-3993 or fax 317-572-4002.

For technical support please visit www.wiley.com/techsupport.

Permissions

Scott Fisher
www.flickr.com/photos/sbfisher

Brianna Stuart
www.stuartphotography.net

Wiley Publishing, Inc.

Praise for Visual Books

"Like a lot of other people, I understand things best when I see them visually. Your books really make learning easy and life more fun."

John T. Frey (Cadillac, MI)

"I have quite a few of your Visual books and have been very pleased with all of them. I love the way the lessons are presented!"

Mary Jane Newman (Yorba Linda, CA)

"I just purchased my third Visual book (my first two are dog-eared now!), and, once again, your product has surpassed my expectations.

Tracey Moore (Memphis, TN)

"I am an avid fan of your Visual books. If I need to learn anything, I just buy one of your books and learn the topic in no time. Wonders! I have even trained my friends to give me Visual books as gifts."

Illona Bergstrom (Aventura, FL)

"Thank you for making it so clear. I appreciate it. I will buy many more Visual books."

J.P. Sangdong (North York, Ontario, Canada)

"I have several books from the Visual series and have always found them to be valuable resources."

Stephen P. Miller (Ballston Spa, NY)

"Thank you for the wonderful books you produce. It wasn't until I was an adult that I discovered how I learn – visually. Nothing compares to Visual books. I love the simple layout. I can just grab a book and use it at my computer, lesson by lesson. And I understand the material! You really know the way I think and learn. Thanks so much!"

Stacey Han (Avondale, AZ)

"I absolutely admire your company's work. Your books are terrific. The format is perfect, especially for visual learners like me. Keep them coming!"

Frederick A. Taylor, Jr. (New Port Richey, FL)

"I have several of your Visual books and they are the best I have ever used."

Stanley Clark (Crawfordville, FL)

"I bought my first Teach Yourself VISUALLY book last month. Wow. Now I want to learn everything in this easy format!"

Tom Vial (New York, NY)

"Thank you, thank you, thank you...for making it so easy for me to break into this high-tech world. I now own four of your books. I recommend them to anyone who is a beginner like myself."

Gay O'Donnell (Calgary, Alberta, Canada)

"I write to extend my thanks and appreciation for your books. They are clear, easy to follow, and straight to the point. Keep up the good work! I bought several of your books and they are just right! No regrets! I will always buy your books because they are the best."

Seward Kollie (Dakar, Senegal)

"Compliments to the chef!! Your books are extraordinary! Or, simply put, extra-ordinary, meaning way above the rest! THANK YOU THANK YOU THANK YOU! I buy them for friends, family, and colleagues."

Christine J. Manfrin (Castle Rock, CO)

"What fantastic teaching books you have produced! Congratulations to you and your staff. You deserve the Nobel Prize in Education in the Software category. Thanks for helping me understand computers."

Bruno Tonon (Melbourne, Australia)

"Over time, I have bought a number of your 'Read Less - Learn More' books. For me, they are THE way to learn anything easily. I learn easiest using your method of teaching."

José A. Mazón (Cuba, NY)

"I am an avid purchaser and reader of the Visual series, and they are the greatest computer books I've seen. The Visual books are perfect for people like myself who enjoy the computer, but want to know how to use it more efficiently. Your books have definitely given me a greater understanding of my computer, and have taught me to use it more effectively. Thank you very much for the hard work, effort, and dedication that you put into this series."

Alex Diaz (Las Vegas, NV)

Credits

Project Editor
Sarah Hellert

Sr. Acquisitions Editor
Jody Lefevere

Copy Editor
Scott Tullis

Technical Editor
Dennis R. Cohen

Editorial Manager
Robyn Siesky

Business Manager
Amy Knies

Sr. Marketing Manager
Sandy Smith

Editorial Assistant
Laura Sinise

Media Development Project Manager
Laura Moss

Media Development Assistant Project Manager
Jenny Swisher

Manufacturing
Allan Conley
Linda Cook
Paul Gilchrist
Jennifer Guynn

Book Design
Kathie Rickard

Project Coordinator
Erin Smith

Layout
Andrea Hornberger
Jennifer Mayberry

Screen Artists
Ana Carrillo
Jill A. Proll

Illustrators
Ronda David-Burroughs
Cheryl Grubbs

Proofreader
Cindy Ballew

Quality Control
David Faust

Indexer
Johanna Van Hoose

Vice President and Executive Group Publisher
Richard Swadley

Vice President and Executive Publisher
Barry Pruett

Composition Director
Debbie Stailey

About the Authors

Mike Wooldridge is a user-interface designer and Web developer. He has authored more than 20 books for the Visual series.

Linda Wooldridge is a former senior editor at *Macworld*. This is her eighth book in the Visual series.

Authors' Acknowledgments

Mike and Linda thank Sarah Hellert for her top-notch project editing, Dennis Cohen for his knowledgable technical editing, and Scott Tullis for his careful copyediting. They enjoyed working with the Visual crew again! They also thank photographers Scott Fisher and Brianna Stuart for the use of their beautiful photos in the examples. This book is dedicated to their nine-year-old son, who enjoys taking digital photos and video.

Table of Contents

chapter 1 — Getting Started

chapter 2 — Understanding Photoshop Basics

chapter 3 Changing the Size of an Image

chapter 4 Making Selections

Table of Contents

chapter 7 **Adjusting Colors**

Table of Contents

chapter **8** **Working with Layers**

chapter **9** **Applying Layer Styles**

chapter 10 Applying Filters

chapter 11 Drawing Shapes

Table of Contents

chapter 12 — Adding and Manipulating Type

chapter 13 — Automating Your Work

chapter 14 Saving and Printing Images

How to use this book

Do you look at the pictures in a book or newspaper before anything else on a page? Would you rather see an image instead of read about how to do something? Search no further. This book is for you. Opening *Teach Yourself VISUALLY Photoshop CS4* allows you to read less and learn more about the Photoshop.

Who Needs This Book

This book is for a reader who has never used this particular technology or software application. It is also for more computer literate individuals who want to expand their knowledge of the different features that Photoshop has to offer.

Book Organization

Teach Yourself VISUALLY Photoshop CS4 has 14 chapters.

Chapter 1, **Getting Started**, introduces you to Photoshop CS4 and shows you how to open an image.

Chapter 2, **Understanding Photoshop Basics**, shows you how to select tools and fine-tune your workspace.

Chapter 3, **Changing the Size of an Image**, teaches you how to change image sizes and crop your images.

Chapter 4, **Making Selections**, shows you how to select objects in your images using different tools.

Chapter 5, **Manipulating Selections**, demonstrates how to change the size and shape of objects in your image after you have selected them.

Chapter 6, **Painting and Drawing with Color**, teaches you how to apply color to your image using the brush and other tools.

Chapter 7, **Adjusting Colors**, shows you how to fine-tune or fix color tones in your image.

Chapter 8, **Working with Layers**, introduces you to layers, which allow you separate parts of your image and work with them independently.

Chapter 9, **Applying Layer Styles**, demonstrates how to add special effects to objects that are in layers.

Chapter 10, **Applying Filters**, teaches you how to transform your image using sophisticated commands.

Chapter 11, **Drawing Shapes**, shows you how to create and edit a variety of different types of shapes in your images.

Chapter 12, **Adding and Manipulating Type**, demonstrates how to apply text to your image to decorate and inform.

Chapter 13, **Automating Your Work**, teaches you how to save time by using Photoshop's automated commands.

Chapter 14, **Saving and Printing Images**, shows you how to save images in a variety of formats and print your images.

Chapter Organization

This book consists of sections, all listed in the book's table of contents. A *section* is a set of steps that show you how to complete a specific computer task.

Each section, usually contained on two facing pages, has an introduction to the task at hand, a set of full-color screen shots and steps that walk you through the task, and a set of tips. This format allows you to quickly look at a topic of interest and learn it instantly.

Chapters group together three or more sections with a common theme. A chapter may also contain pages that give you the background information needed to understand the sections in a chapter.

What You Need to Use This Book

To install and run Photoshop, you need a computer with the following:

- For PCs, an Intel Xeon, Xeon Dual, Centrino, or Pentium 4 processor. For Macs, a PowerPC G4 or G5 processor or Intel-based processor.
- For PCs, Windows XP with Service Pack 2 or higher, Windows Vista, or Windows Server 2008. For Macs, OS X version 10.3, 10.4, or Leopard (10.5).
- Color monitor with a 1024 x 768 monitor resolution and 16-bit video card. 64MB of video RAM.
- 320MB of RAM (384MB recommended).
- For PCs, 650MB of available hard-disk space. For Macs, 1.5GB of available hard-disk space.
- CD-ROM or DVD-ROM drive.
- Internet or phone connection required for product activation.

You may find the following useful for capturing digital photos to use in Photoshop:

- Digital camera
- Image scanner
- Digital camcorder

Using the Mouse

This book uses the following conventions to describe the actions you perform when using the mouse:

Click

Press your left mouse button once. You generally click your mouse on something to select something on the screen.

Double-click

Press your left mouse button twice. Double-clicking something on the computer screen generally opens whatever item you have double-clicked.

Right-click

Press your right mouse button. When you right-click anything on the computer screen, the program displays a shortcut menu containing commands specific to the selected item.

Click and Drag, and Release the Mouse

Move your mouse pointer and hover it over an item on the screen. Press and hold down the left mouse button. Now, move the mouse to where you want to place the item and then release the button. You use this method to move an item from one area of the computer screen to another.

The Conventions in This Book

A number of typographic and layout styles have been used throughout *Teach Yourself VISUALLY Photoshop CS4* to distinguish different types of information.

Bold

Bold type represents the names of commands and options that you interact with. Bold type also indicates text and numbers that you must type into a dialog box or window.

Italics

Italic words introduce a new term and are followed by a definition.

Numbered Steps

You must perform the instructions in numbered steps in order to successfully complete a section and achieve the final results.

Bulleted Steps

These steps point out various optional features. You do not have to perform these steps; they simply give additional information about a feature.

Indented Text

Indented text tells you what the program does in response to you following a numbered step. For example, if you click a certain menu command, a dialog box may appear, or a window may open. Indented text may also tell you what the final result is when you follow a set of numbered steps.

Notes

Notes give additional information. They may describe special conditions that may occur during an operation. They may warn you of a situation that you want to avoid, for example the loss of data. A note may also cross reference a related area of the book. A cross reference may guide you to another chapter, or another section with the current chapter.

Icons and buttons

Icons and buttons are graphical representations within the text. They show you exactly what you need to click to perform a step.

 You can easily identify the tips in any section by looking for the TIPS icon. Tips offer additional information, including tips, hints, and tricks. You can use tips to go beyond what you have learned in the steps.

Operating System Differences

The screen shots used in this book were captured using the Windows Vista operating system. The interfaces features shown in the tasks may differ slightly if you are using a Windows XP or earlier operating system. For example, the default folder for saving photos in Windows Vista is named "Pictures" whereas the default folder in Windows XP for saving photos is named "My Pictures."

Photoshop on a Mac generally works the same as in Windows. We note significant differences between the two platforms in the text and list special Mac key commands in parentheses.

What's on the Web Site

The images used in the book are available online at www.wiley.com/go/photoshopcs4tyv. You can download the images using a Web browser, open them in Photoshop, and then re-create the examples.

Getting Started

Are you interested in creating, modifying, combining, and optimizing digital images on your computer? This chapter introduces you to Adobe Photoshop, a popular software application for working with digital images.

Photoshop enables you to create, modify, combine, and optimize digital images. You can then save the images to print, share via e-mail, publish online, or view on a hand-held device, such as an iPod.

Manipulate Photos

As its name suggests, Photoshop excels at editing digital photographs. You can use the program to make subtle changes, such as adjusting the color in a digital photo or scanned print, or you can use its elaborate filters to make your snapshots look like abstract art. See Chapter 7 for more about adjusting color and Chapter 10 for more about filters.

Paint Pictures

Photoshop's painting features make it a formidable illustration tool as well as a photo editor. You can apply colors or patterns to your images with a variety of brush styles. See Chapter 6 for more about applying color. In addition, you can use the program's typographic tools to integrate stylized letters and words into your images. See Chapter 12 for more about type. You can also create geometric shapes, which are covered in Chapter 11.

Create a Digital Collage

You can combine different image elements in Photoshop. Your compositions can include photos, scanned art, text, and anything else you can save on your computer as a digital image. By placing elements in Photoshop onto separate layers, you can move, transform, and customize them independently of one another. See Chapter 8 for more about layers.

Access, Organize, and Display Photos

Photoshop's Bridge interface offers an easy-to-use tool to access and preview images that are stored on your computer. See the section "Browse for an Image in Bridge" in this chapter. With Bridge, you can easily tag your images with descriptive information, such as where or when they were taken. You can then use that information to sort your photos. Photoshop also offers useful ways to display your images after you edit them. You can display them as a group in a Web photo gallery or combine several sequential images into a single panorama. See Chapter 13 for details.

Put Your Images to Work

After you edit your work, you can utilize your images in a variety of ways. Photoshop lets you print your images, save them in a format suitable for placement on a Web page or e-mailing, or prepare them for use in a page-layout program. See Chapter 14 for more about saving images in different formats as well as printing them.

Understanding Photoshop

Photoshop's tools let you move, color, stylize, and add text to your images. You can optimize the contrast and lighting in photographs or turn them into interesting works of art by applying filters.

Understanding Pixels

Digital images in Photoshop consist of tiny, solid-color squares called *pixels*. Photoshop works its magic by rearranging and recoloring these squares. If you zoom in close, you can see the pixels that make up your image. For more about the Zoom tool, see Chapter 2.

Choose Your Pixels

To edit specific pixels in your image, you first must select them by using one of Photoshop's selection tools. You can make geometric selections using the Marquee, or free-form selections using the Lasso tool. See Chapter 4 for more about the selection tools. Photoshop also has a number of commands that help you select specific parts of your image, such as a certain color or range of colors. Special brushes in Photoshop enable you to select objects in your image based on how the colors of those objects contrast with the background.

Paint

After selecting your pixels, you can apply color to them by using Photoshop's Brush, Airbrush, Paint Bucket, and Pencil tools. You can also fill your selections with solid or semitransparent colors, patterns, or pixels copied from another part of your image. Painting is covered in Chapter 6. Special painting tools help you seamlessly cover up objects in your image, or eliminate dust specks, tears, and other imperfections from a scanned picture.

Adjust Color

You can brighten, darken, and change the hue of colors in parts of your image with Photoshop's Dodge, Burn, and similar tools. Other commands display interactive dialog boxes that let you make wholesale color adjustments, so you can correct overly dark or light digital photographs. See Chapter 7 for details.

Apply Styles and Filters

Photoshop's layer styles let you easily add drop shadows, frame borders, and other effects to your images. You can also perform complex color manipulations or distortions by using filters. Filters can make your image look like an impressionist painting, sharpen or blur your image, or distort your image in various ways. Chapters 9 and 10 cover effects and filters.

Add Type

Photoshop's type tools make it easy to apply titles and labels to your images. You can combine these tools with the program's special effects commands to create warped, 3-D, or wildly colored type. You can find out more about type in Chapter 12.

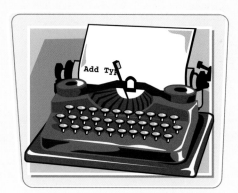

Start Photoshop on a PC

You can start Photoshop on a PC and begin creating and editing digital images.

Start Photoshop on a PC

1 Click **Start**.

2 Click **All Programs** (**All Programs** changes to **Back**).

3 Click **Adobe Photoshop CS4**.

Note: Your path to the Photoshop program may be different, depending on how you installed your software.

Photoshop starts.

Note: To learn how to open an image and start working, see "Open an Image" in this chapter.

Start Photoshop on a Mac

You can start Photoshop on a Mac and begin creating and editing digital images.

Start Photoshop on a Mac

1. In the Finder, click **Applications**.

2. Click the Adobe Photoshop CS4 folder.

3. Double-click the Adobe Photoshop CS4 icon.

Note: *The exact location of the Adobe Photoshop icon may be different, depending on how you installed your software.*

Photoshop starts.

Note: *To learn how to open an image and start working, see "Open an Image" in this chapter.*

The Photoshop Workspace

In Photoshop, you open your digital images in a main image window and use a combination of tools, menu commands, and panel-based features to edit the images.

Application bar

Displays menus that contain most of Photoshop's commands and functions. Special icon-based menus allow you to change the layout of the program. The application bar becomes a single row on wider monitor settings.

Options bar

Displays controls that let you customize the selected tool in the toolbox.

Title tab

Displays the name, magnification, and color mode of an open image. You can switch between images by clicking their respective tabs.

Image window

Displays the images you open in Photoshop.

Panels

Small windows that give you access to common commands and resources. You can click the tabs and icons to display and hide panels.

Toolbox

Displays a variety of icons, each one representing an image-editing tool. You click and drag inside your image to apply most of the tools. Also displays the current foreground and background colors.

Status bar

Displays the magnification of the current image and the amount of computer memory that image is taking up.

Find Images for Your Projects

You can get raw material to work with in Photoshop from a variety of sources.

Start from Scratch

You can create your Photoshop image from scratch by opening a blank canvas in the image window. Then you can apply color and patterns with Photoshop's painting tools or cut and paste parts of other images to create a composite. See the section "Create a New Image" for more about opening a blank canvas.

Digital Camera Photos

Digital cameras are a great way to get digital images onto your computer. Most digital cameras save their images in JPEG or TIFF format, both of which you can open and edit in Photoshop. The program's color adjustment tools are great for correcting color and exposure flaws in digital camera images.

Scanned Photos and Art

A scanner gives you an inexpensive way to convert existing paper- or slide-based content into digital form. You can scan photos and art into your computer, retouch and stylize them in Photoshop, and then output them to a color printer. To automatically separate photos that were scanned together as a single image, see Chapter 3.

Affordable Online Photos

There are many Web sites that feature images that are in the public domain or are available for non-commercial use. Wikimedia Commons (http://commons.wikimedia.org) is one such site. If you have a little money to spend, you can license images from *microstock* Web sites, which are known for low-cost, downloadable images. iStockPhoto (www.istockphoto.com) is a popular microstock site.

Set Preferences

Photoshop's Preferences dialog boxes let you change default settings and customize how the program looks.

Set Preferences

① Click **Edit** (**Photoshop** on a Mac).

② Click **Preferences**.

③ Click **General**.

The Preferences dialog box appears and displays General options.

④ Click here to select which dialog box appears when you select a color.

⑤ Select the general options you want to use (☐ changes to ☑).

⑥ Click **Cursors**.

The Cursors Preferences options appear.

⑦ Select a cursor type to use for the painting tools – the Brush, Eraser, and others (◎ changes to ⦿).

⑧ Select a cursor type to use for the other tools (◎ changes to ⦿).

⑨ Click **Units & Rulers**.

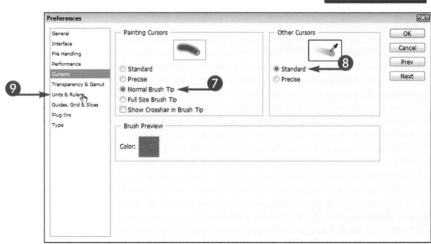

The Units & Rulers Preferences options appear.

⑩ Click here to select the units for the window rulers.

These units become the default units selected when you resize an image.

⑪ Click here to select the default units for type.

⑫ Click **OK**.

Photoshop sets preferences to your specifications.

TIPS

What type of measurement units should I use in Photoshop?

You should use the units most applicable to the type of output you intend to produce. Pixel units are useful for Web imaging because monitor dimensions are measured in pixels. Inches, centimeters, and picas are useful for print because those are standards for working on paper. You can set this under the Units & Rulers preferences.

How can I change the number of operations saved in the History panel?

You can backtrack through your work using the History panel. To change the number of operations Photoshop remembers, click **Performance** in the Preferences window and change the History States value. Photoshop can remember as many as 1000 operations. The default is 20.

Save a Workspace

You can position the different Photoshop panels, define keyboard shortcuts, and customize your menus, then save the arrangement as a workspace. This can be helpful if you work on various types of Photoshop projects that require the use of different tools and commands.

Save a Workspace

SAVE A WORKSPACE

① Arrange the toolbox and panels in the Photoshop interface.

To define keyboard shortcuts or customize menus, click **Edit** and then **Keyboard Shortcuts** or **Menus**.

② Click **Window**.

③ Click **Workspace**.

④ Click **Save Workspace**.

● You can also click the **Essentials** menu to save a workspace.

The Save Workspace dialog box appears.

⑤ Type a name for your workspace.

⑥ Select the interface elements you want to save (□ changes to ☑).

⑦ Click **Save**.

Photoshop saves the workspace.

SELECT A WORKSPACE

① Click **Window**.

② Click **Workspace**.

③ Click a workspace.

You can choose a workspace you have defined previously or only of Photoshop's predefined workspaces.

Photoshop rearranges the workspace.

How do I return to the default workspace?
Follow these steps:

① Click **Window**.

② Click **Workspace**.

③ Click **Essentials (Default)**.

Photoshop returns you to the default setup, with the toolbox on the left side and panels on the right.

● You can click **Delete Workspace** to get rid of a workspace you have saved.

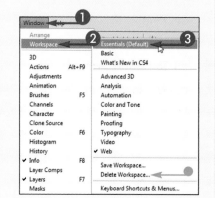

Photoshop comes with plenty of electronic documentation that you can access in case you ever need help.

Get Help

1 Click **Help**.

2 Click **Photoshop Help**.

You can also press F1 (⌘+/ on a Mac) to access Photoshop Help.

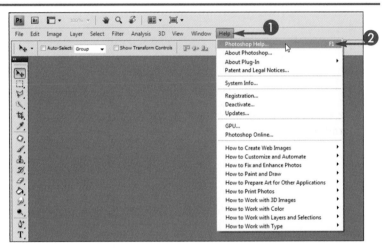

The Adobe Photoshop CS4 Web site opens in your computer's default Web browser.

3 Click a plus icon (⊟ changes to ⊞) to see more specific topics.

4 Click a topic to view its information.

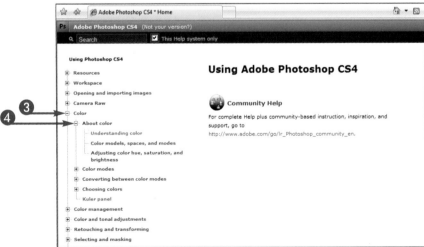

The topic appears in the browser.

- You can click the previous or next icon (◀ or ▶) to go to the previous or next topic in the help system.

⑤ Type a topic in the search box.

⑥ Press Enter.

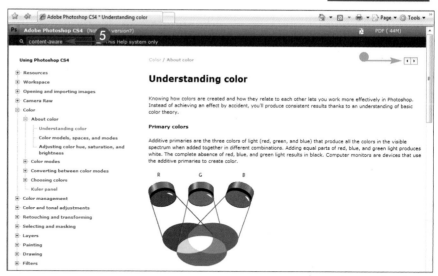

An Adobe search results page appears with a list of relevant topics.

⑦ Click a topic to see the information.

How can I use my Photoshop software on another computer?

Photoshop CS4 requires you to activate your software before using it. Activation involves connecting to Adobe via the Internet to confirm that you have a legitimate copy of Photoshop and are not running the software on multiple computers. To move your copy of Photoshop to another computer, you need to deactivate the software by clicking **Help** and then **Deactivate**. Transferring activation disables the copy of Photoshop on your current computer and allows you to activate a copy of the same software on a different computer after installing it.

Open an Image

You can open an existing image file in Photoshop to modify it or use it in a project.

OPEN AN EXISTING IMAGE

1 Click **File**.

2 Click **Open**.

The Open dialog box appears.

3 Click here to choose the type of files to display in the window.

All Formats is the default, and displays all image and non-image formats.

④ Click here to browse to the folder that contains the image you want to open.

⑤ Click the image you want to open.

⑥ Click **Open**.

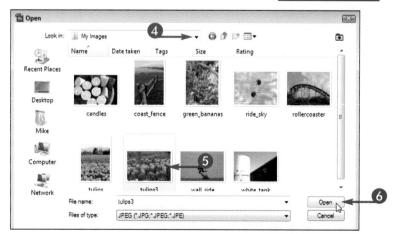

Photoshop opens the image in a window.

● The file name appears in a title tab.

You can specify that images open in floating windows instead of with tabs in the interface preferences.

Note: *For more about preferences, see "Set Preferences."*

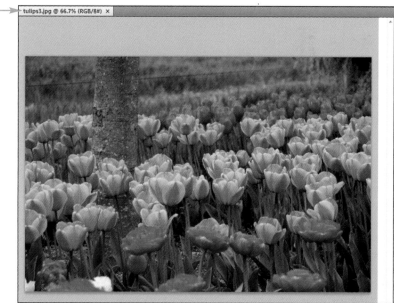

TIP

How do I open a recently accessed image?

① Click **File**.

② Click **Open Recent**.

A list of recently opened files appears.

③ Click the image's file name.

Photoshop opens the image.

Browse for an Image in Bridge

You can open an existing image file by using the Adobe Bridge file browser. Bridge offers a user-friendly way to find and open your images.

In Bridge, you can also add descriptive information to your images and sort them. See the tasks that follow in this chapter for more information.

Browse for an Image in Bridge

① Click **File**.

② Click **Browse in Bridge**.

● You can also click the **Launch Bridge** button (📷).

The Adobe Bridge file browser opens.

③ Click the **Folders** tab.

④ Click ▶ to open folders on your computer (▶ changes to ▼).

⑤ Click a folder on your computer to browse.

The folders and files inside the folder appear.

6 Click an image.

● A preview and information about the image appear.

In this example, the right panel has been widened slightly to show more image information.

7 Double-click the image file to open it.

The image opens.

TIPS

How do I add a rating or label to an image in Bridge?

In Bridge, click the image to select it, click **Label**, and then click a star rating or color label. You can apply a rating of from one to five stars or a text label such as "approve" or "reject." Applying ratings or labels to your images enables you to later sort them by rating or label in the Bridge interface. See the section "Sort and Filter Images in Bridge" for more information.

How can I easily access my image folders in Bridge?

You can mark particular folders where you store your images as Favorites in Bridge. To access the Favorites list, click the Favorites tab in the top left corner of Bridge. To mark a folder as a Favorite, click the folder in the right side of the Bridge window and drag it to the Favorites list. A name and icon for that folder appears. You can remove a favorite by right-clicking it in the menu and selecting **Remove from Favorites**.

Sort and Filter Images in Bridge

You can sort your images by file name, date, file size, dimensions, and other characteristics in Bridge. This can be helpful when you are dealing with hundreds or thousands of images in a collection and need to find a particular image quickly. You can also filter the information displayed in Bridge, specifying that it show only images with a particular rating or label.

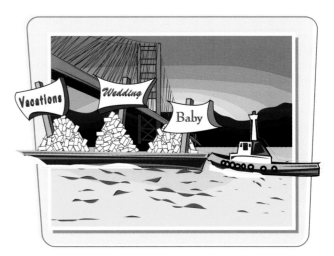

Sort and Filter Images in Bridge

SORT IMAGES

1 Open Adobe Bridge.

2 Click a folder to display its contents.

Note: For details, see the section "Browse for an Image in Bridge."

3 Click **View**.

4 Click **Sort**.

5 Click a category by which to sort.

Bridge sorts the images.

● You can also sort images using the Sort by menu.

FILTER IMAGES

① Click a category by which to filter your images (▶ changes to ▼).

Photoshop displays filter options for the category.

Note: For details about applying ratings, labels, and other categories, see the section "Browse for an Image in Bridge."

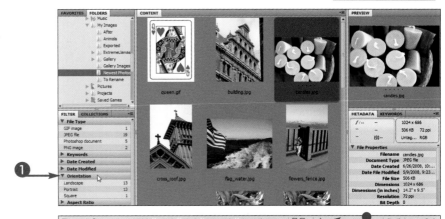

② Click a filter option.

Bridge filters the images, hiding those that are not relevant.

● A check mark appears next to the clicked filter option.

● You can filter by a rating by clicking **Filter Items by Rating** (☆).

TIPS

How can I hide folders and nonimage files in Bridge so that only images are displayed?

To hide folders, click **View** and then **Show Folders**. The check mark next to the Show Folders menu item disappears, and Bridge hides the folders in the right side of the window. To hide nonimage files as well, click **View** and then **Show Graphic Files Only**.

What image-editing functions can I perform in Bridge?

You can rotate images 90 degrees by clicking (rotate counterclockwise) or (rotate clockwise). You can delete images by selecting them and clicking. To perform more-complex editing, you can return to Photoshop by clicking **File** and then **Return to Adobe Photoshop CS3**.

Display a Slideshow in Bridge

You can view a set of images in a folder as a slideshow in Adobe Bridge. You can control the cycling of the slideshow images using keyboard commands.

Display a Slideshow in Bridge

1 Open Adobe Bridge.

2 Click a folder containing the slideshow images.

Note: For details, see the section "Browse for an Image in Bridge."

3 Click **View**.

4 Click **Slideshow Options**.

The Slideshow Options window appears.

You can specify the duration between slides, alignment, and other settings.

5 Click **Play** to open the first slide.

Note: On a Mac, the position of the Play and Done buttons are reversed in the Slideshow Options window.

Bridge starts the slideshow and cycles through the photos in the selected folder.

● You can press **Spacebar** to pause and resume the slideshow.

The sort order in Bridge determines the order of the photos.

Note: See the section "Sort and Filter Images in Bridge" for details.

6 Press **H**.

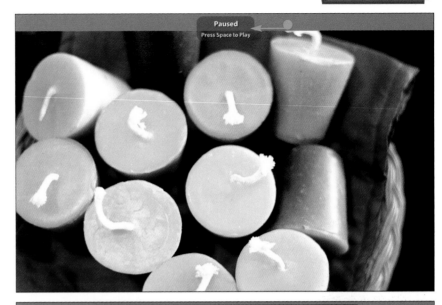

● Bridge displays the slideshow keyboard commands.

7 Press **Esc**.

The slideshow ends.

How can I group similar images in Bridge?

You can group similar images together in Bridge, and free up screen space, by creating a stack.

1 Select the images you want to stack.

2 Click **Stacks**.

3 Click **Group as Stack**.

Bridge creates a single thumbnail for the stack and displays the number of images in the stack.

● You can click the number to reveal the stacked images.

Note: You can select the stack, click **Stacks,** and then click **Ungroup from Stack** to ungroup the images.

Create a New Image

You can start a Photoshop project by creating a blank image.

① Click **File**.

② Click **New**.

The New dialog box appears.

③ Type a name for the new image.

● You can click here to select a preset image size.

④ Type the dimensions and resolution you want.

Note: *For more about dimensions and resolution, see Chapter 3.*

⑤ Click **OK**.

Photoshop creates a new image window at the specified dimensions.

● The image name appears in the title tab.

⑥ Use Photoshop's tools and commands to create your image.

Note: *To learn how to save your image, see Chapter 14.*

Exit Photoshop

You can exit Photoshop after you finish using the application.

Exit Photoshop

EXIT PHOTOSHOP ON A PC

① Click **File**.

② Click **Exit**.

Photoshop closes.

Before exiting, Photoshop alerts you to any open images that have unsaved changes so you can save them.

Note: See Chapter 14 to learn how to save image files.

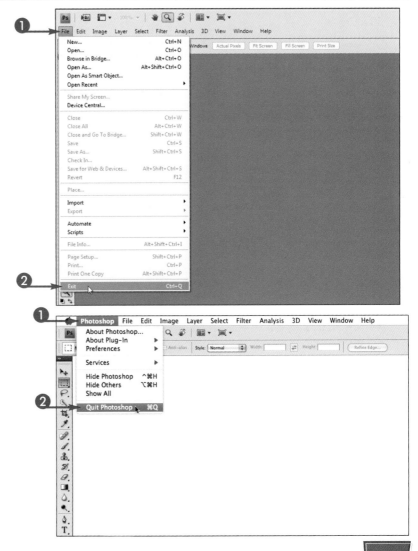

EXIT PHOTOSHOP ON A MAC

① Click **Photoshop**.

② Click **Quit Photoshop**.

Photoshop closes.

Before exiting, Photoshop alerts you to any open images that have unsaved changes so you can save them.

Note: See Chapter 14 to learn how to save image files.

Understanding Photoshop Basics

Are you ready to start working with images? This chapter shows you how to select tools and fine-tune your workspace.

Introducing the Photoshop Toolbox

To help you manipulate photos, Photoshop offers a variety of specialized tools that let you edit your image. Take some time to familiarize yourself with the toolbox tools.

You can select tools by clicking buttons in the toolbox or by typing a keyboard shortcut key. Keyboard shortcut keys are shown in parentheses.

Move (V)

Moves selected areas of an image.

Marquee (M)

Selects pixels by drawing a box or circle around the area you want to edit.

Lasso (L)

Selects pixels by drawing a free-form shape around the area you want to edit.

Quick Selection Brush (W)

Selects pixels using brush shapes.

Crop (C)

Trims an image to create a new size.

Eyedropper (K)

Samples color from an area of an image.

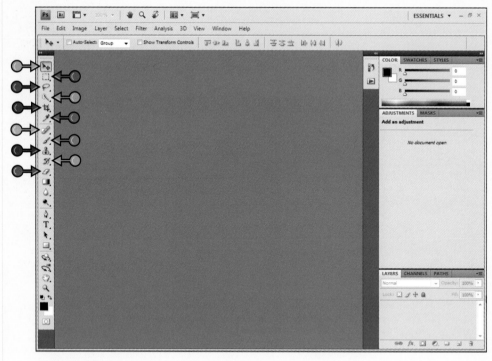

Spot Healing Brush (J)

Quickly fixes slight imperfections by cloning nearby pixels.

Brush (B)

Paints strokes of color.

Clone Stamp (S)

Duplicates an area of the image.

History Brush (Y)

Paints a previous state of your image onto the current image.

Eraser (E)

Erases pixels.

Gradient (G)

Fills selected areas with blended color effects.

Blur (R)

Blurs objects in your image.

Dodge (O)

Brightens specific areas of your image.

Pen (P)

Creates custom shapes by drawing and connecting lines, or paths.

Type (T)

Adds type to an image or selects type that you have added.

Path Selection (A)

Selects lines that you have drawn with the pen or other tools.

Rectangle (U)

Draws solid, rectangular shapes.

3D Tools

Creates and edits 3D objects. (These tools are available only in the Extended version of Photoshop and are not covered in this book.)

Hand (H)

Shifts an image in the image window to display unseen parts.

Zoom (Z)

Zooms your view of an image in or out.

Foreground and Background Color

Displays and lets you set foreground and background colors.

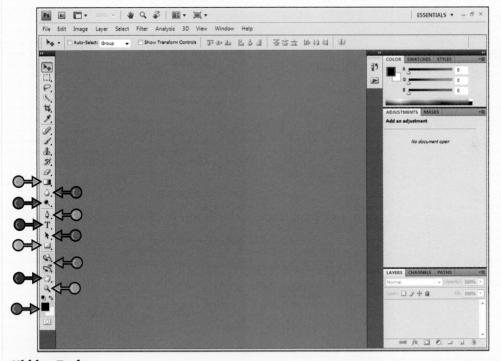

Hidden Tools

Tool buttons that include a small triangle (▣) in the corner have hidden tools located beneath them. Click and hold a tool button to access the hidden tools. For example, the Lasso has a Polygonal Lasso and Magnetic Lasso hidden beneath it. You can cycle through hidden tools beneath a tool by typing the shortcut key for that tool repeatedly.

Work with Toolbox Tools

You can use the tools in Photoshop's toolbox to make changes to an image. Positioning the mouse pointer over a tool displays the tool name. After you click to select a tool, the options bar displays controls for customizing how the tool works. Some tools include a small triangle in the corner indicating hidden tools you can select.

Work with Toolbox Tools

SELECT A TOOL

1 Position the mouse pointer over a tool.

● A label appears displaying the tool name. You can click the tool name to access Help information about the tool.

2 Click a tool to select it.

The options bar displays customizing options for the selected tool.

3 Specify any options you want for the tool.

SELECT A HIDDEN TOOL

1 Click a tool that has a triangle in its corner.

2 Press and hold the mouse button.

Note: You can also right-click the tool.

A menu of hidden tools appears.

3 Click the tool you want to use.

REARRANGE THE TOOLBOX

1 Click .

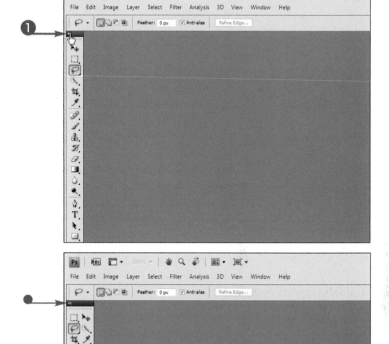

● Photoshop rearranges the toolbox tools into two columns.

● You can click ◄◄ to switch back to a single column.

TIPS

How do I float the toolbox?

You can float the toolbox to drag it to a more convenient place on the screen. To float the toolbox, click and drag the title bar of the toolbox. You can unfloat the toolbox by dragging it back to near the left edge of the screen. When you release the mouse button, Photoshop docks the toolbox to the left edge.

How do I close the toolbox?

Closing the toolbox frees up space in the Photoshop interface. To close the toolbox, click **Window**, and then click **Tools**. To reopen the toolbox, click **Window** and then **Tools** again. You can also press Tab to open or close the toolbox as well as all panels.

Magnify with the Zoom Tool

You can change the magnification of an image with the Zoom tool. With this tool, you can view small details in an image or view an image at full size.

Magnify with the Zoom Tool

INCREASE MAGNIFICATION

1. Click the **Zoom** tool (🔍).

- You can also access the Zoom tool in the application bar.

  ⬚ changes to ⊕.

2. Click the image.

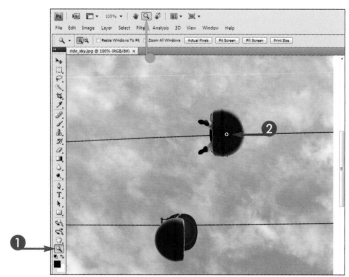

Photoshop increases the magnification of the image.

The point that you click in the image is centered in the window.

The current magnification shows in the title tab and status bar.

- You can choose an exact magnification by typing a percentage value in the status bar.

DECREASE MAGNIFICATION

① Click the **Zoom Out** icon (🔍).

  ⬚ changes to 🔍.

② Click the image.

  Photoshop decreases the magnification of the image.

  The current magnification shows in the title bar and status bar.

  You can also press and hold **Alt** (**Option** on a Mac) and click the image to decrease magnification.

MAGNIFY A DETAIL

① Click the **Zoom In** icon (🔍).

② Click and drag with the Zoom tool to select the detail.

  The object appears enlarged on-screen.

TIP

How do I quickly return an image to 100% magnification?

The following are seven different ways to return the image to 100% magnification:

① By double-clicking the **Zoom** tool (🔍).

② By clicking **Actual Pixels** on the options bar.

③ By clicking **View** and then **Actual Pixels** from the menu.

④ By selecting **100%** from the application bar menu.

⑤ By typing **100%** in the lower left corner of the image window.

⑥ By right-clicking the image and selecting **Actual Pixels** from the menu that appears.

⑦ By pressing **Ctrl**+**1** (**⌘**+**1** on a Mac).

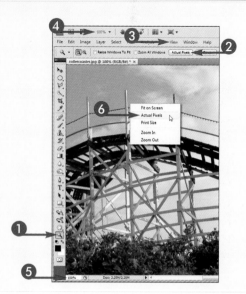

Adjust Views

You can move an image within the window by using the Hand tool or scroll bars. The Hand tool helps you navigate to an exact area on the image.

The Hand tool is a more flexible alternative to using the scroll bars because, unlike the scroll bars, the Hand tool enables you to drag the image freely in two dimensions.

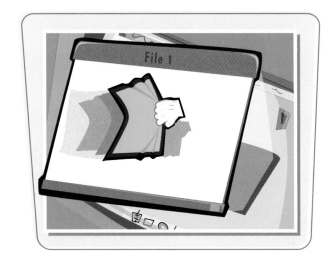

USING THE HAND TOOL

1 Click the **Hand** tool (🖐).

● You can also access the Hand tool in the application bar.

Note: For 🖐 to produce an effect, the image must extend outside the boundary of the image window.

2 Click **Window**.

3 Click **Navigator**.

● The Navigator panel opens to show your current view relative to the entire image.

🔖 changes to 🖐.

4 Click and drag inside the image window.

The view of the image shifts inside the window.

● The Navigator panel shows the changed view.

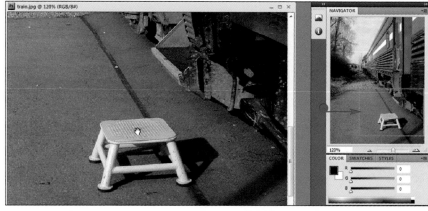

USING THE SCROLL BARS

① Click and hold one of the window's scroll bar buttons.

The image scrolls.

TIP

How can I quickly adjust the image window to see the entire image at its largest possible magnification on-screen?

The following are six different ways to magnify the image to its largest possible size:

① By double-clicking the **Hand** tool (🖑).
② By clicking **Fit Screen** on the options bar.
③ By clicking **View** and then **Fit on Screen** from the menu.
④ By selecting **Fit on Screen** from the application bar menu (or the main menu bar on a Mac).
⑤ By right-clicking the image and selecting **Fit on Screen** from the menu that appears.
⑥ By pressing Ctrl+0 (⌘+0 on a Mac).

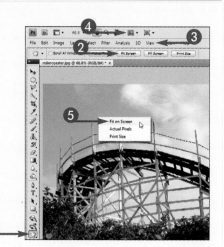

Change Screen Modes

You can switch the screen mode to change the look of your workspace on-screen and give yourself more room to view your current image.

In the standard screen mode, you can view multiple images at the same time, each in a different window.

SWITCH TO FULL SCREEN MODE WITH MENU BAR

1 Click the **Screen Mode** icon (▣).

2 From the list that appears, click **Full Screen Mode With Menu Bar**.

Photoshop maximizes the size of the image in the workspace between the toolbox and the panels.

The title tab and status bar are not visible. If you have multiple images open, you can switch between them in the Window menu.

SWITCH TO FULL SCREEN MODE

1 Click ▣.

2 From the list that appears, click **Full Screen Mode**.

3 If a dialog box appears explaining Full Screen Mode, click **Full Screen** to close it.

The image appears full screen alone without the menu bar, options bar, toolbox, or panels.

You can press F or Esc to return to Standard Screen Mode.

You can press Tab to open the toolbox and panels.

Note: Pressing Tab hides and shows the toolbox and panels in all of Photoshop's screen modes.

Is there a shortcut for changing screen modes?

Press F to cycle through the screen modes using your keyboard. To cycle through in opposite order, press Shift+F.

How do I change tools while in Full Screen Mode?

You can open the toolbox by pressing Tab or you can press a shortcut key. Here are shortcut keys for the more popular tools. For a complete list, see "Introducing the Photoshop Toolbox."

Marquee	M
Move	V
Lasso	L
Brush	B
Type	T
Zoom	Z
Eraser	E
Quick Selection tool	W

Using Rulers and Guides

You can turn on rulers and create guides to help place elements accurately in your image.

Guides help you align elements in your image with one another. These lines do not appear on the printed image.

Using Rulers and Guides

VIEW RULERS AND GUIDES

1 Click **View**.

2 Click **Rulers**.

Note: To change the units of measurement on rulers and make other preference changes, see Chapter 1.

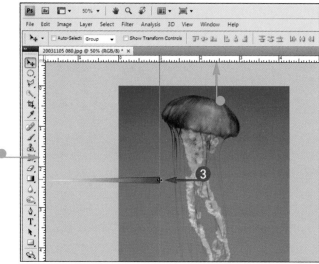

● Photoshop adds rulers to the top and left sides of the image window.

3 Click one of the rulers and drag the cursor into the window (⬚ changes to ⬦).

You can drag the top ruler down to create a horizontal guide.

You can drag the left ruler to the right to create a vertical guide.

● A thin, colored line called a guide appears.

You can also click **View** and then **New Guide** to add a guide.

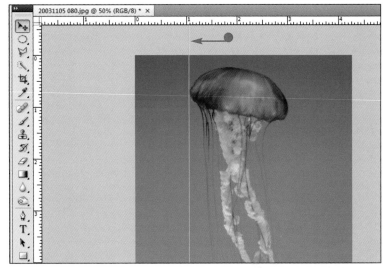

MOVE A GUIDE

1 Click the **Move** tool ().

2 Place your cursor over a guide (changes to ⊹).

3 Click a guide and drag it to a new position.

TIP

How do I make objects in my images "snap to" my guides when I move those objects?

The "snap to" feature can be useful when you want to align elements in a row horizontally or in a column vertically.

1 Click **View**.

2 Click **Snap To**.

3 Click **Guides**.

● When you move an object, Photoshop automatically snaps it to any nearby guides.

Note: For more about layers, see Chapter 8.

Undo Commands

You can undo multiple commands using the History panel. This enables you to correct mistakes or change your mind about operations you have performed on your image.

The History panel lists recently executed commands with the most recent command at the bottom.

Undo Commands

1 Click **Window**.

2 Click **History**.

The History panel opens.

3 Click the **History** slider ([D]) and drag it upward.

● Alternatively, you can click a previous command in the History panel.

● Photoshop undoes the previous commands.

● You can click and drag [D] down to redo the commands.

Revert an Image

You can revert an image to the
previously saved state and begin
editing your image again.

Revert an Image

1 Click **File**.

2 Click **Revert**.

Photoshop reverts the image to
its previously saved state.

You can click **Edit** and then **Undo
Revert** to return to the
unreverted state.

Manage Image Windows

Each image you open in Photoshop appears in its own window. Windows can take up the entire workspace and you can select between different ones by clicking tabs. You can also float or tile windows so you can see content from more than one window at once. This can be useful if you are copying content between them.

Work with Image Windows

① Open two or more images.

Note: *For details about opening images, see Chapter 1.*

● The active, or current, image appears here.

By default, the different open images are distinguished by tabs.

② Click the tab for the image you want to view.

You can also select your images from a list at the bottom of the Window menu.

● The image you select appears as the active image.

③ Click **Window**.

④ Click **Arrange**.

⑤ Click **Float in Window**.

Photoshop displays the active image in a floating window.

● You can click and drag the title bar to move the window.

⑥ Click **Window**.

⑦ Click **Arrange**.

⑧ Click **Tile**.

Photoshop tiles the windows so that all images are visible.

● You can click and drag here to resize the window.

Note: To copy content between two open windows, see Chapter 5.

You can click **Window** and then **Consolidate All to Tabs** to return to the windows to tabs.

TIPS

How can I make the views consistent between different open images?

You can click **Window**, **Arrange**, and then **Match Zoom** to set the zoom levels of all the open images to that of the active image. You can click **Window**, **Arrange**, and then **Match Location** to make the viewing location consistent across all open images. To match both zoom and location, click **Window**, **Arrange**, and then **Match All**.

Are there shortcuts for managing tabbed windows?

Yes. You can right-click a window's tab to access a menu of commands. The commands include Close for closing that tab's image, Close All for closing all the currently open images, and Open Document for opening a new image.

Changing the Size of an Image

You can change the size of your image to make it fit on a Web page or in a printed document. This chapter shows you how to change the on-screen or print size and print resolution as well as how to crop an image.

Change the On-Screen Size of an Image

You can change the size at which an image displays on your computer monitor so that viewers can see the entire image. To change the on-screen size, Photoshop adjusts the number of pixels that make up the image.

Because you lose less sharpness when you decrease an image's size than when you increase it, consider starting with an image that is too big rather than one that is too small.

Change the On-Screen Size of an Image

① Click **Image**.

② Click **Image Size**.

● The Image Size dialog box appears, listing the height and width of the image.

③ Make sure **Resample Image** is selected (☐ changes to ☑) to change the number of pixels in the image.

Changing the number of pixels changes the on-screen size.

④ Type a size for a dimension.

● To resize by a certain percentage, click here and change the units to percent.

● Select **Constrain Proportions** (☐ changes to ☑), if it is not already selected, to force the other dimension to change proportionally.

● You can restore the original dialog box settings by pressing and holding Alt (Option on a Mac) and clicking **Cancel**, which changes to **Reset**.

⑤ Click **OK**.

Photoshop resizes the image.

Note: *Increasing the number of pixels in an image can add blur. To sharpen a resized image, apply the Unsharp Mask filter as covered in Chapter 10.*

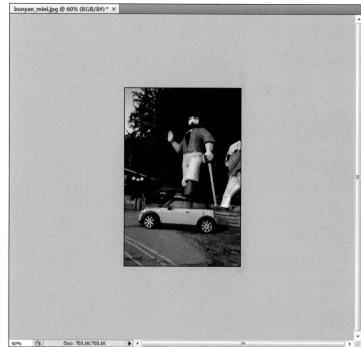

TIP

How do I change the size of an image as I am saving it for the Web?

You can change the size in the Save for Web & Devices dialog box.

① Click **File** and then click **Save for Web & Devices**.

② Type a new value in the W or H field to change the dimensions of your image.

● You can also change the size of your image by a percentage.

③ Click **Save**.

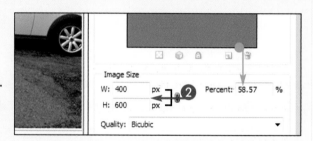

Change the Print Size of an Image

You can change the printed size of an image to determine how it appears on paper. The printed size of an image depends on the number of pixels in the image and the resolution, which measures the pixel density on the printed page.

① Click **Image**.

② Click **Image Size**.

● The Image Size dialog box appears, listing the current height and width of the printed image.

● You can click here to change the unit of measurement.

③ Type a size for a dimension.

● You can select **Constrain Proportions** (☐ changes to ☑), if it is not already selected, to force the other dimension to change proportionally.

● You can restore the original dialog box settings by pressing and holding **Alt** (**Option** on a Mac) and clicking **Cancel**, which changes to **Reset**.

④ Click **OK**.

Photoshop resizes the image.

Note: Changing the number of pixels in an image can add blur. To sharpen a resized image, apply the Unsharp Mask filter as covered in Chapter 10.

TIP

How do I preview an image's printed size?

Follow these steps:

① Click **File** and then click **Print**.

● A dialog box displays how the image will print on the page.

● Other options let you adjust the size and positioning of the image.

Note: For more information on printing images, see Chapter 14.

Change the Resolution of an Image

You can change the print resolution of an image to increase or decrease the print quality.

The resolution, combined with the number of pixels in the image, determines the size of a printed image.

The greater the resolution, the better the image looks on the printed page — up to a limit, which varies with the type of printer and paper quality.

1 Click **Image**.

2 Click **Image Size**.

● The Image Size dialog box appears, listing the current resolution of the image.

3 Make sure **Resample Image** is selected (changes to) to change the number of pixels in the image as you adjust the resolution.

● You can click here to change the resolution units.

④ Type a new resolution.

● You can restore the original
dialog box settings by pressing
and holding **Alt** (**Option** on a
Mac) and clicking **Cancel**, which
changes to **Reset**.

⑤ Click **OK**.

In this example, adjusting the
resolution changes the number of
pixels in the image. The on-screen
image becomes larger or smaller,
while the print size stays the
same.

TIPS

What is the relationship between resolution, on-screen size, and print size?

To determine the printed size of a
Photoshop image, you can
divide the on-screen size by the
resolution. If you have an image
with an on-screen width of
480 pixels and a resolution of
120 pixels per inch, the
printed width is 4 inches.

How can I use the Measure tool to measure dimensions in my image?

Click and hold the **Eyedropper** tool ( ) and
select the **Measure** tool ( ). You can then click
and drag inside your image to
measure the dimensions of
objects. Click **Window** and then
Info to open the Info panel and
see your measurements. You can
change the Info panel units in
the Units & Rulers preferences. See
Chapter 1 for details about changing preferences.

Crop an Image

You can use the Crop tool to change the size of an image by removing unneeded space on the top, bottom, and sides.

CROP ONLY

① Click the **Crop** tool (⊬).

   ⳗ changes to ⊬.

② Click and drag ⊬ to select the area of the image you want to keep.

   You can also crop an image by changing its canvas size or by selecting with the Rectangular Marquee tool and selecting **Image** and then **Crop**.

Note: *See the section "Change the Canvas Size of an Image" for more information.*

③ Click and drag the side and corner handles (☐) to adjust the size of the cropping boundary.

   You can click and drag inside the cropping boundary to move it without adjusting its size.

● To exit without cropping the image, you can click ⊘ or press Esc to cancel.

④ To accept, click ✓ or press Enter (⌘+Return on a Mac).

Photoshop crops the image, deleting the pixels outside the cropping boundary.

ROTATE AND CROP

1 Perform Steps **1** to **3** on the previous page.

2 Click and drag outside the boundary lines.

3 To accept, click ✓ or press Enter (⌘+Return on a Mac).

Photoshop rotates the image and crops it.

TIP

How can I constrain the dimensions of the Crop tool?

Perform the following steps:

1 Type the width and height of the cropping boundary in the options bar.

● You can also specify a resolution in the options bar.

2 Drag 🔲 to apply the Crop tool.

Photoshop constrains the rectangle to the specified dimensions.

Crop and Straighten Photos

You can automatically crop and straighten one or more photographs in a Photoshop image. After cropping and straightening, Photoshop places each image in its own image window. This feature is useful if you digitize several images at the same time on a scanner and want to separate them.

The feature works best when the images to be cropped and straightened contrast with the background.

Crop and Straighten Photos

1 Click **File**.

2 Click **Automate**.

3 Click **Crop and Straighten Photos**.

● Photoshop straightens the photos, crops out any blank space, and copies the photos to separate image windows.

Note: *To learn how to save newly cropped images, see Chapter 14.*

● The original image remains in its own window.

Trim an Image

Trim an Image

You can use the Trim command to automatically remove any blank space surrounding your image. This can be useful for scanned photos or when you want to minimize the file size of an image. Options let you trim space from all four sides, or just some of them.

The feature works best when the image to be trimmed contrasts with the background.

Trim an Image

1 Click **Image**.

2 Click **Trim**.

The Trim dialog box appears.

3 Specify how to select the type of pixels you want to trim (○ changes to ◉).

4 Select the areas to trim (☐ changes to ☑).

5 Click **OK**.

Photoshop trims the image.

Change the Canvas Size of an Image

You can alter the canvas size of an image in order to change its rectangular shape or to add blank space around its borders.

The *canvas* is the area on which an image sits. Changing the canvas size is one way to crop an image.

The Crop tool provides an alternative to changing the canvas size. See the section "Crop an Image" for more information.

Change the Canvas Size of an Image

① Click **Image**.

② Click **Canvas Size**.

- The Canvas Size dialog box appears, listing the current dimensions of the canvas.

- You can click here to change the unit of measurement.

③ Type the new canvas dimensions.

● You can modify in what directions Photoshop changes the canvas size by clicking an anchor point.

● You can specify the color with which Photoshop fills any new canvas area if you enlarge a dimension.

④ Click **OK**.

*Note: If you decrease a dimension, Photoshop displays a dialog box asking whether you want to proceed. Click **Proceed**.*

Photoshop changes the image's canvas size.

Because the middle anchor point is selected in this example, the canvas size changes equally on opposite sides.

How do I increase the area of an image using the Crop tool?

You can enlarge the image window to add extra space around the image. Then you can apply the **Crop** tool (🔲) so that the cropping boundary extends beyond the borders of the image. When you apply cropping, the image canvas enlarges. Photoshop applies the current background color in the new space. For more about selecting colors, see Chapter 6.

How can I crop without making the image canvas smaller?

Use a selection tool, such as the Rectangular Marquee tool (▢), to select a cropping boundary. Click **Select** and then **Inverse** to select the area outside the boundary. Pressing Backspace (Delete on a Mac) crops the image but keeps your canvas dimensions the same. If you are working with a multilayer image, this technique crops content only in the selected layer.

Making Selections

You can move, color, or transform parts of your image independently from the rest of the image. The first step is to make a selection. This chapter shows you how.

Select with the Marquee Tools

You can select a rectangular or elliptical area of your image by using the Marquee tools. Then you can move, delete, or stylize the selected area using other Photoshop commands.

Select with the Marquee Tools

USING THE RECTANGULAR MARQUEE TOOL

① Click the **Rectangular Marquee** tool (▭).

⟍ changes to ✛.

② Click and drag diagonally inside the image window.

You can press and hold **Shift** while you click and drag to create a square selection.

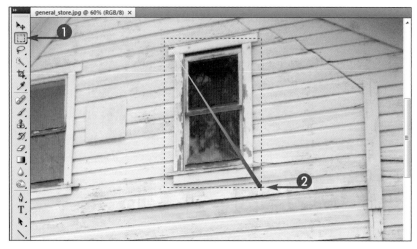

● Photoshop selects a rectangular portion of your image. You can now perform other commands on the selection.

● You can deselect a selection by clicking **Select** and then **Deselect**.

62

USING THE ELLIPTICAL MARQUEE TOOL

1 Click and hold ▣.

2 From the list that appears, click the **Elliptical Marquee** tool (◯).

   ▷ changes to ＋.

3 Click and drag diagonally inside the image window.

   You can press and hold **Shift** while you click and drag to create a circular selection and press **Alt** (**Option**) to draw the circle directly out from the center.

● Photoshop selects an elliptical portion of your image.

   You can now perform other commands on the selection.

   You can deselect a selection by clicking **Select** and then **Deselect**.

 TIP

How do I customize the Marquee tools?
Use the text fields and menus in the options bar:

● **Feather:** The Feather value softens your selection edge, which means that Photoshop partially selects pixels near the edge.

● **Style:** Define your Marquee tool as a fixed size or fixed aspect ratio.

● **Height and Width:** Add an exact width and height for a fixed-size selection or a ratio for a fixed-aspect-ratio selection by entering values in the Width and Height boxes. These boxes are editable when you select a fixed-size or fixed-aspect-ratio marquee.

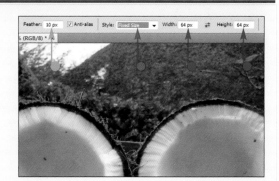

Select with the Lasso Tool

You can create oddly shaped selections with the Lasso tools. Then you can move, delete, or stylize the selected area using other Photoshop commands.

You can use the regular Lasso tool to create curved or jagged selections. With the Polygonal Lasso tool, you can easily create a selection made up of many straight lines.

Select with the Lasso Tool

USING THE REGULAR LASSO

1 Click the **Lasso** tool (⌷).

2 Click and drag your cursor (⌷) to make a selection.

● To accurately trace a complicated edge, you can magnify that part of the image with the Zoom tool (🔍).

Note: See Chapter 2 for more about the Zoom tool.

3 Drag to the beginning point and release the mouse button.

The selection is complete.

USING THE POLYGONAL LASSO

1 Click and hold .

2 From the list that appears, click the **Polygonal Lasso** tool (☒).

☒ changes to ☒.

3 Click multiple times along the border of the area you want to select.

4 To complete the selection, click the starting point.

You can also double-click anywhere in the image and Photoshop adds a final straight line connected to the starting point.

The selection is complete.

You can achieve a polygonal effect with the regular Lasso tool by pressing Alt (Option on a Mac) and clicking to make your selection.

TIP

What if my lasso selection is not as precise as I want it to be?
Selecting complicated outlines with ☒ can be difficult, even for the steadiest of hands. To fix an imprecise Lasso selection, you can:

● Deselect the selection, by clicking **Select** and then **Deselect**, and try again.

● Try to fix your selection. See the section "Add To or Subtract From a Selection."

● Switch to the Magnetic Lasso tool (☒). See the section "Select with the Magnetic Lasso Tool."

Select with the Magnetic Lasso Tool

You can select elements of your image that have well-defined edges quickly and easily with the Magnetic Lasso tool.

The Magnetic Lasso works best when the element you try to select contrasts sharply with the surrounding content.

Select with the Magnetic Lasso Tool

① Click and hold ⊘.

② Click the **Magnetic Lasso** tool (⊠) from the list that appears.

③ Click the edge of the object you want to select.

This creates a beginning anchor point, which is a fixed point on the lasso path.

④ Drag your cursor (⊠) along the edge of the object.

The Magnetic Lasso's path snaps to the edge of the element as you drag.

● To help guide the lasso, you can click to add anchor points as you go along the path.

You can press Delete to remove the most recently added anchor point. This allows you to restructure a lasso path that is incorrect.

⑤ Click the beginning anchor point to finish your selection.

Alternatively, you can double-click anywhere in the image and Photoshop completes the selection for you.

The path is complete.

This example shows that the Magnetic Lasso is less useful for selecting areas where you find little contrast between the image and its background.

How can I adjust the precision of the Magnetic Lasso tool?
Use the options bar:

● **Width:** The number of nearby pixels the lasso considers when creating a selection. If you magnify the edge you are selecting, you can typically decrease the width.

● **Contrast:** How much contrast is required for the lasso to consider something an edge. Decrease the edge contrast to select fuzzier edges.

● **Frequency:** The frequency of the anchor points. Increase the frequency for better precision when selecting poorly defined edges.

Select with the Quick Selection Tool

You can paint selections onto your images using the Quick Selection tool. This tool offers a quick way to select objects that have solid colors and well-defined edges.

You can adjust the brush size of the tool to fine-tune your selections.

Select with the Quick Selection Tool

① Click the **Quick Selection** tool (🖌️).

② Click ▾ to open the tool's Brush menu.

The Brush menu opens.

In the Brush menu, you can specify the tool's size and other characteristics. Decreasing the tool's hardness causes it to partially select pixels at the perimeter.

③ Click and drag inside the object you want to select.

- Photoshop selects parts of the object based on its coloring and the contrast of its edges.

- After you make a selection, the Add to Selection button (⟨⟩) becomes active.

4️⃣ Click and drag to select more of the object.

- Photoshop adds to the selection.

TIP

How can I adjust the selection made with the Quick Selection tool?

1️⃣ In the options bar, click **Refine Edge**.

The Refine Edge window appears, and Photoshop turns the unselected part of your image white.

- Increase Contrast to heighten the sharpness of the selection edges.

- Increase Feather to make the selection edges partially transparent.

- Use Contract/Expand to decrease or increase the selection slightly.

Select with the Magic Wand Tool

You can select groups of similarly colored pixels with the Magic Wand tool. You may find this useful if you want to remove an object from a background.

You can control how precisely the tool makes the selection by choosing a tolerance value from 0 to 255.

Select with the Magic Wand Tool

1. Click and hold the **Quick Selection** tool ().

2. Click the **Magic Wand** tool.

3. Type a number from 0 to 255 in the Tolerance field.

   To select a narrow range of colors, type a small number; to select a wide range of colors, type a large number.

4. Click the cursor in the area you want to select inside the image.

   Photoshop selects the pixel you clicked, plus any similarly colored pixels near it.

5 To add to your selection, press **Shift** and click elsewhere in the image.

● You can also click the **Add to Selection** button (▣) in the options bar.

Photoshop adds to your selection.

● You can click the **Subtract from Selection** button (▣) to configure the Magic Wand to remove selected pixels

Note: For more details, see "Add To or Subtract From a Selection."

6 To delete the selected pixels, press **Delete**.

● Photoshop replaces the pixels with the background color, or makes them transparent if you made the selection in a layer.

In this example, Photoshop replaces the pixels with white.

Note: See Chapter 8 for more about layers.

How can I ensure that the Magic Wand tool selects all the occurrences of a color in an image?

You can deselect **Contiguous** (☑ changes to ☐) in the options bar so that the Magic Wand tool selects similar colors, even when they are not contiguous with the pixel you click with the tool. This can be useful when objects intersect the solid-color areas of your image. You can also select **Sample All Layers** (☐ changes to ☑) to select similar colors in all layers in the image, not just the currently selected layer.

Select with the Color Range Command

You can select a set range of colors within an image with the Color Range command. With this command, you can quickly select a region of relatively solid color, such as a sky or a blank wall.

① Click **Select**.

② Click **Color Range**.

The Color Range dialog box appears.

⟍ changes to ⟍.

③ Click inside the image window.

● Photoshop selects all the pixels in the image that are similar to the pixel you clicked. These areas turn white in the Color Range window.

● The number of pixels that turn white depends on the Fuzziness setting.

4 To increase the range of color, click and drag the **Fuzziness** slider () to the right.

You can decrease the color range by dragging the slider to the left.

● You can broaden the selected area by clicking the **Add** eyedropper (🖋) and then clicking other parts of the image.

5 Click **OK**.

Photoshop makes the selection in the main image window.

Note: *Sometimes the Color Range command selects unwanted areas of the image. To eliminate these areas, see the section "Add To or Subtract From a Selection."*

TIP

How do I limit the area of the image that the Color Range command affects?

Select an area of the image — by using the Marquee, Lasso, or another tool — before clicking **Select** and then **Color Range**.

Select All the Pixels in an Image

You can select all the pixels in a single-layer image by using the Select All command. With the entire image window selected, you can easily delete the image, or copy and paste it into another window.

For multilayer images, Select All selects all the pixels in the currently selected layer.

1 Click **Select**.

2 Click **All**.

You can also press Ctrl + A (⌘ + A on a Mac) to select all the pixels.

● Photoshop selects the entire image window.

You can delete the currently selected pixels by pressing Delete.

To copy your image, press Ctrl + C (⌘ + C on a Mac).

To paste your image, press Ctrl + V (⌘ + V on a Mac).

Move a Selection Border

You can move a selection border if your original selection is not in the intended place.

Move a Selection Border

① Make a selection using one of Photoshop's selection tools ([▭], [◯], or [⤫]).

● Make sure the New Selection button ([▢]) is highlighted.

② Click and drag inside the selection.

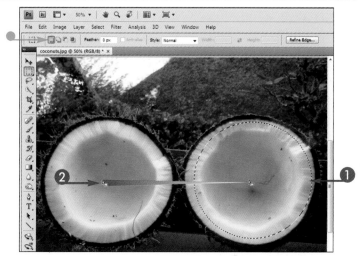

● The selection border moves.

To move your selection one pixel at a time, you can use the arrow keys on your keyboard.

You can hide a selection by clicking **View**, **Show**, and then **Selection Edges**.

Add To or Subtract From a Selection

You can add to or subtract from your selection by using various selection tools.

Add To or Subtract From a Selection

ADD TO A SELECTION

1 Make a selection using one of Photoshop's selection tools ([▣], [◯], or [✦]).

2 Click a selection tool.

This example uses the Magnetic Lasso tool ([✦]).

Note: *See the previous sections in this chapter to select the appropriate tool for your image.*

3 Click the **Add to Selection** button ([▣]).

4 Select the area you want to add.

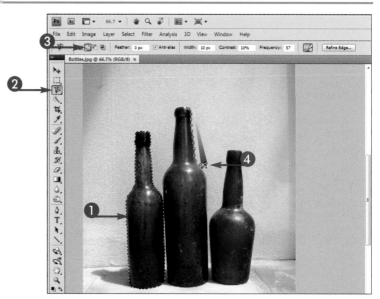

5 Complete the selection.

● Photoshop adds to the selection.

You can enlarge the selection further by repeating Steps **2** to **5**.

You can also add to a selection by pressing **Shift** as you make your selection.

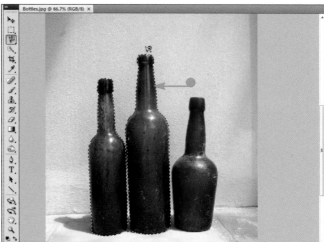

SUBTRACT FROM A SELECTION

1 Make a selection using one of Photoshop's selection tools.

2 Click a selection tool.

This example uses the Rectangular Marquee tool (□).

3 Click the **Subtract from Selection** button (□).

4 Select the area you want to subtract.

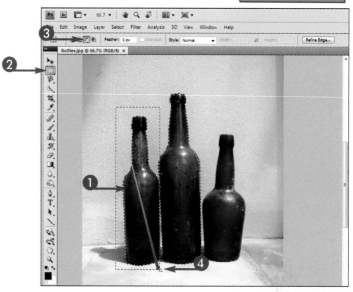

● Photoshop deselects, or subtracts, the selected area.

You can subtract other parts of the selection by repeating Steps **2** to **4**.

You can also subtract from a selection by pressing and holding **Alt** (**Option** on a Mac) as you make your selection.

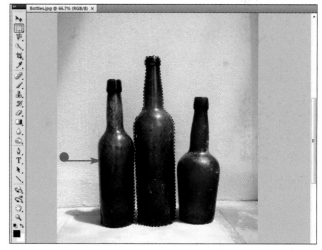

TIPS

How do I add to or subtract from a selection using the Quick Selection tool?

The Quick Selection tool features different option buttons for adding to or subtracting from a selection. In the options bar, you can click to add to a selection and to subtract from a selection.

How can I expand or contract a selection?

To expand a selection, click **Select**, **Modify**, and then **Expand**. A dialog box appears, enabling you to specify the amount of expansion in pixels. To contract a selection, click **Select**, **Modify**, and then **Contract**. A dialog box appears, enabling you to specify the amount of contraction in pixels.

Invert a Selection

You can invert a selection to deselect what is currently selected and select everything else. This is useful when you want to select the background around an object.

Invert a Selection

① Make a selection using one of Photoshop's selection tools.

Note: *For more about the various selection tools, see the previous sections in this chapter.*

② Click **Select**.

③ Click **Inverse**.

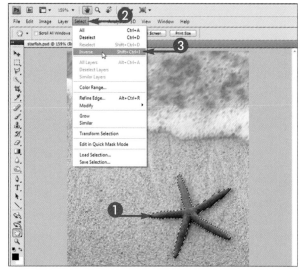

Photoshop inverts the selection.

78

Grow a Selection

You can increase the size of your selection using the Grow command, which is useful when you want to include similarly colored, neighboring pixels in your selection.

Grow a Selection

1. Make a selection using one of Photoshop's selection tools.

Note: To learn more about the various selection tools, see the previous sections in this chapter.

2. Click **Select**.

3. Click **Grow**.

● The selection grows to include similarly colored pixels contiguous with the current selection.

● To include noncontiguous pixels as well, you can click **Select** and then **Similar**.

● You can change the number of similarly colored pixels the Grow command selects by changing the Tolerance setting; click [icon], type a new number in the Tolerance field, make your selection, and click **Select** and then **Grow**.

Create Slices

You can divide a large image that you want to display on the Web into smaller rectangular sections called *slices*. The different slices of an image can then be optimized independently of one another for faster download. See Chapter 14 for details.

① Click and hold the **Crop** tool 🔲.

② Click the **Slice** tool (✂) from the list that appears.

    ↳ changes to ✂.

③ Click and drag inside the image to create a slice.

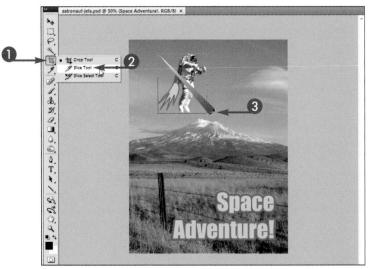

● Photoshop creates a slice where you clicked and dragged.

Note: Slices you define are called user slices.

    Photoshop fills in the rest of the image with auto slices.

Note: User slices remain fixed when you add more slices to your image, whereas auto slices can change size.

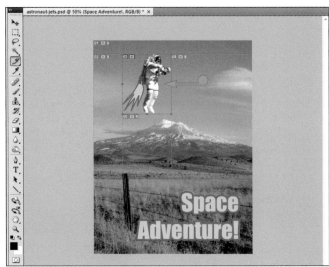

④ Click and drag to define another
slice in your image.

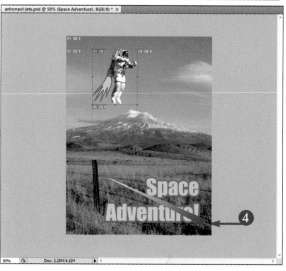

● Photoshop creates another slice
where you click and drag.

Photoshop creates or rearranges
auto slices to fill in the rest of the
image.

Note: *To learn how to save the different slices for
the Web, see Chapter 14.*

Note: *To save a sliced image so you can edit the
slices later, save the image in the Photoshop
format. See Chapter 14 for details.*

How do I resize or delete slices in my image?
First, click the **Slice Select** tool (), which is accessible by clicking
and holding . To resize a user slice, click inside it and then click
and drag a border handle. To delete a user slice, click inside it and
press Delete . When you resize or delete slices, Photoshop
automatically resizes, creates, and deletes auto slices in the image to
account for the change.

Manipulating Selections

Making a selection defines a specific area of your Photoshop image. This chapter shows you how to move, stretch, erase, and manipulate your selections in a variety of ways.

Move a Selection

You can move a selection by using the Move tool, which enables you to rearrange elements of your image.

You can place elements of your image either in the background or in layers. For details about layers, see Chapter 8.

MOVE A SELECTED OBJECT IN THE BACKGROUND

1 Click the Background layer in the Layers panel.

If you start with a newly scanned image, Photoshop makes the Background layer the only layer.

2 Make a selection with a selection tool.

Note: See Chapter 4 for more about the selection tools, and Chapter 8 for more about layers.

3 Click the **Move** tool (⊕).

4 Click inside the selection and drag.

● Photoshop fills the original location of the object with the current background color.

● In this example, white is the default background color.

MOVE A SELECTED OBJECT IN A LAYER

1 Click a non-background layer in the Layers panel.

2 Make a selection with a selection tool.

Note: *See Chapter 4 for more about the selection tools, and Chapter 8 for more about layers.*

3 Click .

4 Click inside the selection and drag.

Photoshop moves the selection in the layer.

Photoshop fills the original location of the object with transparent pixels.

Note: *Unlike the Background — Photoshop's opaque default layer — layers can include transparent pixels.*

TIPS

How do I move a selection in a straight line?

Press and hold Shift while you drag with the **Move** tool (). Doing so constrains the movement of your object horizontally, vertically, or diagonally — depending on the direction you drag.

How do I move several layers at a time?

You can link the layers you want to move, select one of the linked layers, and then move them all with the Move tool. You can also Ctrl+click (⌘+click) to select multiple layers and then move them with the Move tool. For more information, see Chapter 8.

Copy and Paste a Selection

You can copy a selection and make a duplicate of it somewhere else in the image.

Copy and Paste a Selection

USING THE KEYBOARD AND MOUSE

① Make a selection with a selection tool.

Note: See Chapter 4 for more about the selection tools.

② Click ⊞.

③ Press **Alt** (**Option** on a Mac) while you click and drag the object.

④ Release the mouse button to drop the selection.

Photoshop creates a duplicate of the object, which appears in the new location.

USING THE COPY AND PASTE COMMANDS

① Make a selection with a selection tool.

Note: See Chapter 4 for more about the selection tools.

② Click **Edit**.

③ Click **Copy**.

④ Using a selection tool, select where you want to paste the copied element.

If you do not select an area, Photoshop pastes the copy over the original.

⑤ Click **Edit**.

⑥ Click **Paste**.

● Photoshop pastes the copy into a new layer, which you can now move independently of the original image.

Note: See the section "Move a Selection" for more about moving your image.

TIPS

How can I copy a selection from one window to another?

Click and click and drag your selection from one window to another. You can also copy selections between windows using the Copy and Paste commands in the Edit menu. To make multiple windows visible at the same time, see Chapter 2.

How can I copy content from multiple layers at once?

If your selection overlaps several layers in your image, you can click **Edit** and then **Copy Merged** to combine all the content into a single layer. Using the regular Copy command copies only from the selected layer. For more about layers, see Chapter 8.

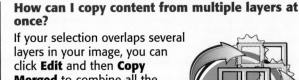

Delete a Selection

You can delete a selection to remove an element from your image.

Delete a Selection

① Make a selection with a selection tool.

Note: *See Chapter 4 for more about the selection tools.*

② Press Delete.

Photoshop deletes the selection.

If you are working in the Background layer, the empty area fills with the background color — in this example, white, the default background color.

If you are working in a layer other than the Background layer, deleting an object turns the selected pixels transparent.

Rotate a Selection

You can rotate a selection to tilt the selected pixels or turn them upside down in your image.

Rotate a Selection

① Make a selection with a selection tool.

Note: See Chapter 4 for more about the selection tools.

② Click **Edit**.

③ Click **Transform**.

④ Click **Rotate**.

A *bounding box*, a rectangular box with handles on the sides and corners, surrounds the object.

⑤ Click and drag to the side of the object.

The object rotates.

Note: You can rotate your selection precisely by typing percentage values in the W and H fields in the options bar.

⑥ To apply the rotation, click ☑ or press Enter (⌘+Return on a Mac).

● To cancel, you can click ⊘ or press Esc.

● In this example, a layer containing an astronaut is rotated.

Note: See Chapter 8 for more about layers.

Scale a Selection

You can scale a selection to make the selected area larger or smaller. By scaling, you can emphasize parts of your image.

Scale a Selection

① Make a selection with a selection tool.

Note: *See Chapter 4 for more about the selection tools.*

② Click **Edit**.

③ Click **Transform**.

④ Click **Scale**.

A rectangular bounding box with handles on the sides and corners surrounds the object.

⑤ Click and drag a corner handle to scale both the horizontal and vertical axes.

Note: *You can scale your selection precisely by typing percentage values in the W and H fields in the options bar.*

6 Click and drag a side handle to scale one axis at a time.

7 To apply the scaling, click ✓ or press Enter (⌘+Return on a Mac).

● To cancel, you can click ⊘ or press Esc.

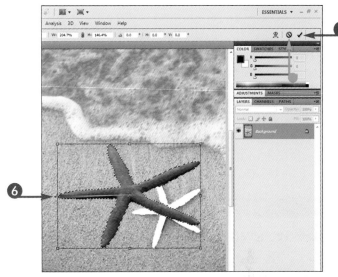

Photoshop scales the object to the new dimensions.

● In this example, an object in the Background layer is scaled.

Note: See Chapter 8 for more about layers.

● The area behind the object is filled with the background color.

 TIPS

How do I scale both dimensions proportionally?

You can press and hold Shift or click **Maintain Aspect Ratio** (⬚) in the options bar. When you scale your selection, the two axes of your selection grow or shrink proportionally; Photoshop does not distort your image.

How can I exactly double the size of my selection?

When scaling your selection, type **200%** in the W (width) and H (height) boxes in the options bar. These boxes enable you to scale your selection to a precise percentage of its original size.

Skew or Distort a Selection

You can transform a selection using the Skew or Distort command. This enables you to stretch a selected area in your image into interesting shapes.

Skew or Distort a Selection

SKEW A SELECTION

1 Make a selection with a selection tool.

Note: See Chapter 4 for more about the selection tools.

2 Click **Edit**.

3 Click **Transform**.

4 Click **Skew**.

● A rectangular bounding box with handles on the sides and corners surrounds the object.

5 Click and drag a handle to skew the object.

Because the Skew command works along a single axis, you can drag either horizontally or vertically.

Note: You can skew your selection precisely by typing percentage values in the W and H fields in the options bar.

6 To apply the skewing, click ✓ or press Enter (⌘+Return on a Mac).

● To cancel, you can click ⊘ or press Esc.

DISTORT A SELECTION

① Make a selection with a selection tool.

Note: See Chapter 4 for more about the selection tools.

② Click **Edit**.

③ Click **Transform**.

④ Click **Distort**.

● A rectangular bounding box with handles on the sides and corners surrounds the object.

⑤ Click and drag a handle to distort the object.

The Distort command works independently of the selection's different axes; you can drag a handle both vertically and horizontally.

Note: You can distort your selection precisely by typing percentage values in the W and H fields in the options bar.

⑥ To apply the distortion, click ✓ or press Enter (⌘+Return on a Mac).

● To cancel, you can click ⊘ or press Esc.

TIPS

How can I undo my skewing or distortion?

You can click **Edit** and then **Undo** to undo the last handle adjustment you made. This is an alternative to clicking ⊘, which cancels the entire Skew or Distort command.

How can I flip my image horizontally or vertically?

You can click **Edit**, Transform, and then **Flip Horizontal** or **Flip Vertical**. The Flip Horizontal command makes a selection look like its mirror image.

Perform Content-Aware Scaling

You can use Photoshop's new content-aware scaling feature to intelligently change the dimensions of an image. Important foreground objects stay the same size while the less important background shrinks or enlarges. This feature works best with landscape and beach photos, where important objects stand out clearly from the rest of the scene. It works less well on more complicated images.

Perform Content-Aware Scaling

1 Click **Select**.

2 Select **All**.

Photoshop selects all the pixels in your image.

3 Click **Edit**.

4 Click **Content-Aware Scale**.

Handles appear on the edges of the selection.

⑤ Click and drag the handles to shrink or enlarge the image.

In this example, the child against the wall remains unchanged while the wall scales smaller.

⑥ To apply the scaling, click ✓ or press Enter (⌘+Return on a Mac).

● To cancel, you can click ⊘ or press Esc.

This shows the same example with the regular scale command applied. All the content in the image changes size equally.

Note: *See "Scale a Selection" for more details.*

 TIP

How can I improve content-aware scaling of images with people in them?

Use the Protect Skin Tones setting to have Photoshop recognize objects with skin tones and selectively protect those objects.

① Follow Steps 1 to 4 above to access content-aware scaling.

② Click **Protect Skin Tones** (👤).

③ Click and drag the handles to scale the image.

If objects in the image have skin color, Photoshop protects them as you scale. In this example, the jumping child is protected while the rock, water, and other background content scales.

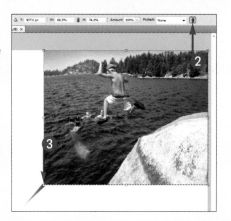

Feather the Border of a Selection

You can feather a selection's border to create soft edges.

To soften edges, select an object, feather the selection border, and then delete the part of the image that surrounds your selection.

Feather the Border of a Selection

SELECT AND FEATHER THE IMAGE

1 Make a selection with a selection tool.

Note: See Chapter 4 for more about the selection tools.

2 Click **Refine Edge**.

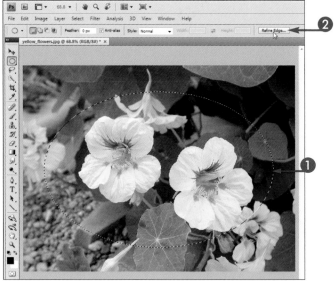

The Refine Edge dialog box appears.

3 Type a pixel value between 0.1 and 250 in the Feather section to determine the softness of the edge.

The larger the number, the thicker the softened edge.

4 Click **OK**.

DELETE THE SURROUNDING BACKGROUND

⑤ Click **Select**.

⑥ Click **Inverse**.

The selection inverts but remains feathered.

⑦ Press Delete.

Photoshop applies the feathering to the image.

TIPS

What happens if I feather a selection and then apply a command to it?

Photoshop applies the command only partially to pixels near the edge of the selection. For example, if you remove color from a selection using the Hue/Saturation command, color at the feathered edge of the selection is only partially removed. For more information about the Hue/Saturation command, see Chapter 7.

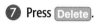

Is there another way to feather my selection?

When selecting with the Marquee or Lasso tool, you can create a feathered selection by first typing a pixel value greater than 0 in the Feather text field in the options bar. Your resulting selection will have a feathered edge.

Create Vanishing Point Planes

You can model the 3-D characteristics of flat objects in your image by creating planes with the Vanishing Point tool. This can be useful if you work with objects such as the sides of buildings, interior walls, or table surfaces.

After you create Vanishing Point planes, you can apply special Photoshop commands. See the section "Copy between Vanishing Point Planes" for details.

Create Vanishing Point Planes

① Open an image that includes flat surfaces.

Note: See Chapter 1 for more about opening an image.

② Click **Filter**.

③ Click **Vanishing Point**.

The Vanishing Point dialog box appears.

④ Click the **Create Plane** tool (▦).

⑤ Click to mark a corner of a plane.

⑥ Click a second time to mark another corner.

Photoshop connects the points to create a plane edge.

⑦ Click two more times to mark the final two corners of the plane.

Photoshop creates the Vanishing Point plane.

● You can use the Edit Plane tool () to move a plane or adjust its corners or sides.

⑧ Click 🔲 to reselect the Create Plane tool.

⑨ Click four more times to create another Vanishing Point plane.

Photoshop creates the Vanishing Point plane, which is oriented differently from the first.

● To delete a plane, you can select a plane with 🔲 and press Delete.

⑩ Click **OK**.

Photoshop saves your work and closes the dialog box.

TIP

Why is it called the Vanishing Point tool?
In perspective drawing, the vanishing point is the point on the horizon where receding parallel lines appear to meet. Photoshop uses such parallel lines to represent the planes in the Vanishing Point dialog box.

Copy between Vanishing Point Planes

You can copy an object between two Vanishing Point planes. Photoshop transforms the object as you move it so that it conforms to the orientation of the current plane.

Copy between Vanishing Point Planes

① Create Vanishing Point planes in your image.

Note: For details, see the section "Create Vanishing Point Planes."

② Click **Filter**.

③ Click **Vanishing Point**.

The Vanishing Point dialog box appears, displaying the different planes.

④ Click the **Marquee** tool (▢).

⑤ Click and drag to select an object inside a plane.

Photoshop draws a marquee whose sides are parallel to those of the plane.

6 Press and hold **Alt** (**Option** on a Mac).

7 Click and drag the selection from one plane to another.

Photoshop transforms the selection to orient it with the destination plane.

8 Click the **Transform** tool ().

9 Select **Flip** (☐ changes to ☑) to flip the selection horizontally.

10 Select **Flop** (☐ changes to ☑) to flip the selection vertically.

11 Click **OK**.

Photoshop saves your work and closes the dialog box.

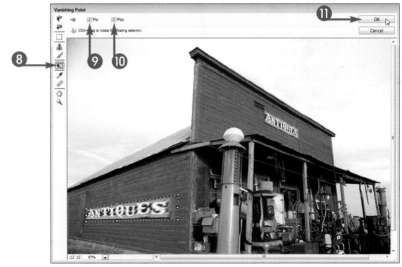

TIPS

What does the Brush tool do in the Vanishing Point dialog box?

Like the normal Brush, it applies the foreground color to objects in your image. But in the Vanishing Point dialog box, the brush shape conforms to the plane in which you paint. You can control the characteristics of the brush with the settings at the top of the dialog box.

What does the Stamp tool do in the Vanishing Point dialog box?

It enables you to clone content from one Vanishing Point plane to another. The cloned pixels conform to the shape of the current plane.

CHAPTER 6

Painting and Drawing with Color

You can add splashes, streaks, or solid areas of color to your image. Photoshop offers a variety of tools with which you can add almost any color imaginable. This chapter introduces you to those tools and shows you how to choose your colors.

Select the Foreground and Background Colors

You can select two colors to work with at a time in Photoshop — a foreground color and a background color. Painting tools such as the Brush apply the foreground color. You apply the background color when you use the Eraser tool on the Background layer, enlarge the image canvas, or cut pieces out of your image.

Select the Foreground and Background Colors

SELECT THE FOREGROUND COLOR

① Click the **Foreground Color** box.

The Color Picker dialog box appears.

● To change the range of colors that appears in the color box, click and drag the slider (⬚◁).

② Click the color you want as the foreground color in the color box.

③ Click **OK**.

● The selected color appears in the Foreground Color box.

④ Click a painting tool in the toolbox.

This example uses the Brush tool (✐).

Note: For more about painting tools, see the section "Using the Brush Tool."

⑤ Click and drag to apply the color.

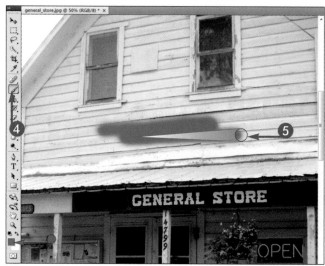

SELECT THE BACKGROUND COLOR

1 Click the **Background Color** box.

The Color Picker dialog box appears.

● To change the range of colors that appears in the color box, click and drag ▷◁.

2 To select a background color, click the color you want in the color box.

3 Click **OK**.

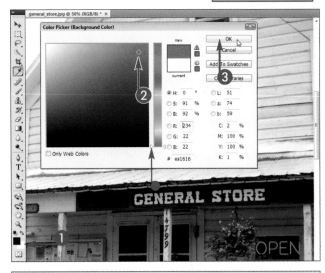

● The selected color appears in the Background Color box.

4 Click the **Eraser** tool (⬜).

5 Click and drag the cursor (○).

The tool erases by painting with the background color.

Note: Painting occurs only when erasing in the Background layer; in other layers, the eraser turns pixels transparent. See Chapter 8 for a full discussion of layers.

 TIPS

How do I reset the foreground and background colors?

Click the **Default** icon (⬛) to the upper left of the Foreground and Background icons. Doing so resets the colors to black and white.

What is a Web-Safe color?

Web browsers on some older monitors can display only colors from a specific 216-color palette. These colors are known as Web-safe colors. You can click **Only Web Colors** in the Color Picker dialog box (⬜ changes to ☑) to restrict your choices to Web-safe colors.

Select a Color with the Eyedropper Tool

You can select a color from an open image with the Eyedropper tool. The Eyedropper tool enables you to paint using a color already present in your image.

① Click the **Eyedropper** tool (🖉).

② Position 🖉 over your image.

● You can click **Window** and then **Info** to open the Info panel to see color values as you move 🖉.

③ Click to select the color of the pixel beneath the tip of 🖉.

● The color becomes the new foreground color.

To select a new background color, you can press Alt (Option on a Mac) as you click in Step **3**.

You can temporarily employ the Eyedropper tool when using a painting tool such as the Brush or Paint Bucket by pressing and holding Alt (Option).

Select a Color with the Swatches Panel

You can select a color with the Swatches panel. The Swatches panel lets you choose from a small set of commonly used colors.

Select a Color with the Swatches Panel

① Click **Window**.

② Click **Swatches**.

● The Swatches panel opens.

③ Position your cursor over a color swatch.

⬚ changes to ⬚.

④ Click a color swatch to select a foreground color.

● The color becomes the new foreground color.

To select a background color, press Alt (Option on a Mac) as you click in Step **3**.

You can use the Eyedropper tool (⬚) to add the current foreground color to the Swatches panel. After selecting the tool, position it over the empty area of the panel and click.

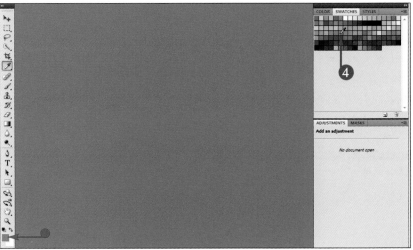

Using the Brush Tool

You can use the Brush tool to add color to your image. You may find the brush useful for applying bands of color.

To limit where the brush applies color, create a selection before painting. For details, see Chapter 4.

For details, see Chapter 4.

Using the Brush Tool

1 Click ✎.

2 Click the **Foreground Color** box to select a color with which to paint.

Note: For details, see the section "Select the Foreground and Background Colors."

3 Click the **Brush** ⏷ and select a brush size and type.

Note: To access different brush styles, see "Change Brush Styles."

4 Click and drag to apply the foreground color to the image.

To undo the most recent brush stroke, you can click **Edit** and then **Undo Brush**.

Note: To undo more than one brush stroke, see Chapter 2 for more about the History panel.

5 Type a percentage value to change the opacity of the brush strokes.

Alternatively, you can click the **Opacity** ▸ and adjust the slider.

6 Click and drag to apply the semitransparent paintbrush.

7 Type a percentage value to change how much color the brush applies.

Alternatively, you can click the **Flow** ▸ and adjust the slider.

8 Click and drag to apply the customized brush.

Photoshop applies color per your specifications.

 TIPS

What are the Pencil and Airbrush tools?

You can use the Pencil tool to draw hard-edged lines of color. To access the Pencil tool, click 🖊 and then 🖉. The Airbrush tool paints soft lines that get darker the longer you hold down your mouse button. You can convert your brush to an airbrush by clicking the **Airbrush** button (🖌) in the options bar.

What is a virtual slider?

You can adjust certain slider-based settings, such as the Opacity and Fill settings in the Layers panel, by positioning the cursor over the setting's label and clicking and dragging. For example, you can hover over **Opacity** and click and drag to the left or right to decrease or increase the currently selected layer's opacity.

Change Brush Styles

You can select from a variety of predefined brush styles to apply color in different ways. The types of brushes available include calligraphic brushes, texture brushes, and brushes that enable you to add drop shadows to objects.

① Click ✎.

② Click the **Brush** ⏷.

③ Click ▶.

The Brush menu appears.

④ Click a set of brushes.

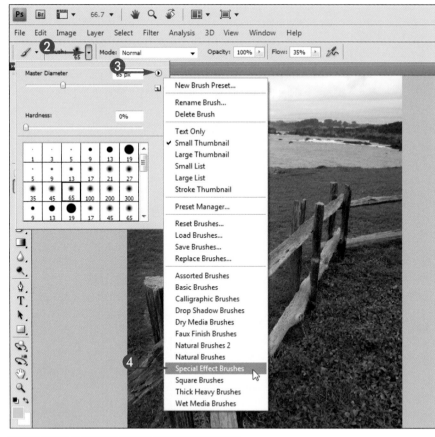

A dialog box appears asking if you want to replace your brushes.

⑤ Click **OK**.

● To add the set of brushes to the currently displayed set, click **Append**.

If a dialog box appears asking if you want to save the current brush set, click **No**.

Note: You can reset your brushes to the original set by selecting **Reset Brushes** from the Brush menu.

The new set appears in the Brush list.

⑥ Click a brush style to select it.

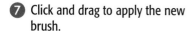

⑦ Click and drag to apply the new brush.

Photoshop applies color with the brush.

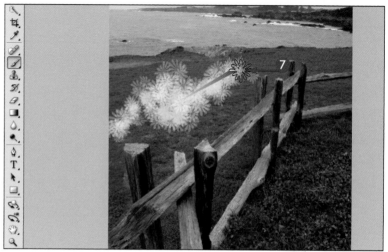

TIP

How can I give my brush strokes a scattered appearance?

① Click **Window** and then **Brushes**.

② In the Brushes panel, click **Scattering** (☐ changes to ☑).

③ Click and drag the **Scatter** slider (△) to the right.

● Photoshop displays an example of the brush stroke.

Create a Custom Brush

You can use the Brushes panel to create one-of-a-kind brushes of varying sizes and shapes. You can even specify a brush shape that changes as it paints, to generate a random design.

Create a Custom Brush

1 Click .

2 Click **Window**.

3 Click **Brushes**.

   The Brushes panel opens.

4 Click **Brush Tip Shape**.

5 Click a brush style to use as a starting point for your custom brush.

6 Click and drag the **Diameter** slider (△) to change the brush size.

7 Type a Roundness value between 0% and 100%.

   The lower the number, the more oval the brush.

   You can adjust other settings to further define the tip shape.

8 Select **Shape Dynamics** (▢ changes to ☑).

9 Click and drag the **Size Jitter** △ to specify the amount your brush varies in size as it paints.

10 Click and drag the **Minimum Diameter** △ to specify the smallest size to which the brush scales when Size Jitter is enabled.

11 Click and drag the other sliders to control how the brush angle and roundness change.

You can click other categories to define other settings.

12 Click ▶▶ to close the Brushes panel.

13 Click and drag inside the image.

Photoshop applies the custom brush.

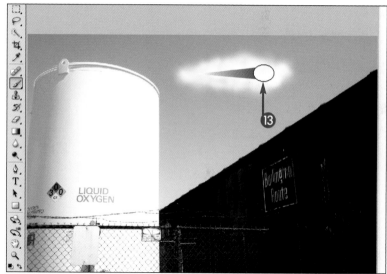

TIP

How do I save my custom brush in the Brush drop-down menu?

1 In the Brushes panel, click ▼≡.
2 Click **New Brush Preset**.
3 Type a name in the Brush Name dialog box.
4 Click **OK**.

Photoshop adds your brush to the Brush menu.

Apply a Gradient

You can apply a *gradient*, which is a transition from one color to another. This can give objects or areas in your image a shaded or 3-D look.

For another way to add a gradient to your image, see Chapter 8.

Apply a Gradient

1. Make a selection.

Note: *See Chapter 4 for more about making selections.*

2. Click the **Gradient** tool (⬛).

● A linear gradient is the default.

You can select different geometries in the options bar.

3. Click the gradient swatch.

The Gradient Editor appears.

4. Select a gradient type from the preset box.

● Photoshop shows the settings for the selected gradient below.

You can customize the gradient using the settings.

5. Click **OK**.

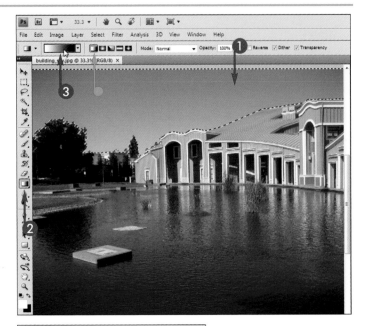

6 Click and drag inside the selection.

The direction and transition of the gradient are defined.

Note: *Dragging a long line with the tool produces a gradual transition; dragging a short line produces an abrupt transition.*

● Photoshop generates a gradient inside the selection.

TIP

How can I customize the colors and opacity of my gradient?

● Click the Color Stops to define the colors in a gradient. To add new gradient colors, click along the bottom of the gradient.

● Click the Opacity Stops to define the transparency of the gradient colors. To add new opacity settings, click along the top of the gradient.

● You can click and drag the Midpoint icon to specify where the gradient's transition occurs.

Using the Paint Bucket Tool

You can fill areas in your image with solid color using the Paint Bucket tool.

The Paint Bucket tool affects only adjacent pixels in the image. You can set the Paint Bucket's Tolerance value to determine what range of colors the paint bucket affects in the image when you apply it.

To fill the pixels of a selected area, rather than just adjacent pixels, see the section "Fill a Selection."

Using the Paint Bucket Tool

ADD COLOR USING THE PAINT BUCKET

1 Click and hold ▣.

2 From the list that appears, click the **Paint Bucket** tool (▧).

   ⊳ changes to ◇.

3 Click the **Foreground Color** box to select a color for painting.

Note: For details, see the section "Select the Foreground and Background Colors."

4 Type a Tolerance value from 0 to 255.

   With a low value, the tool fills only adjacent colors that are very similar to that of the clicked pixel.

   A high value fills a broader range of colors.

5 Click inside the image.

   Photoshop fills that area of the image with the foreground color.

ADJUST OPACITY

6 To fill an area with a semitransparent color, type a percentage value of less than 100 in the Opacity field.

7 Click inside the image.

Photoshop fills an area with see-through paint.

CONSTRAIN THE COLOR

8 To constrain where you apply the color, make a selection before clicking.

In this example, the opacity is reset to 100 percent.

9 Click inside the selection.

The fill effect stays within the boundary of the selection. The tolerance setting also still controls where the effect appears.

TIP

How can I reset a tool to its default settings?
Right-click (Control+click) the tool's icon on the far left side of the options bar and click **Reset Tool** from the menu that appears.

Fill a Selection

You can fill a selection using the Fill command. The Fill command is an alternative to the Paint Bucket tool. The Fill command differs from the Paint Bucket tool in that it fills the entire selected area, not just adjacent pixels based on a tolerance value.

See the section "Using the Paint Bucket Tool" if you want to fill adjacent pixels rather than a selected area.

Fill a Selection

① Define the area you want to fill using a selection tool.

Note: See Chapter 4 for more about using the selection tools.

② Click **Edit**.

③ Click **Fill**.

④ Click here and select a fill option.

● You can also fill your selection with a custom pattern. For details on using this option, see the tip in the section "Using the Pattern Stamp."

● You can decrease the opacity to fill with a semitransparent color or pattern.

⑤ Click **OK**.

● Photoshop fills the area.

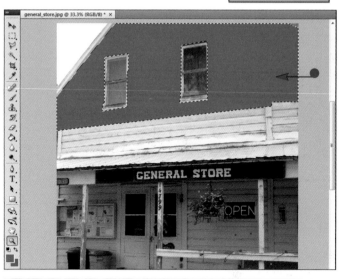

You can select other areas and fill them with different colors.

● This example uses a fill with the background color set to 30 percent opacity and the blending mode set to Hard Light.

Note: For more about blending modes, see Chapter 8.

 TIPS

How do I apply a "ghosted" white covering over part of an image?

Use a selection tool to define the area of the image that you want to cover, and then apply the Fill command with white selected and the opacity set to less than 50 percent.

What does the Preserve Transparency option in the Fill dialog box do?

If you select **Preserve Transparency** (☐ changes to ☑), Photoshop does not fill pixels that are transparent in the selected layer. This option enables you to easily color objects that exist by themselves in a layer. This feature is not available when working in the Background layer.

Stroke a Selection

You can use the Stroke command to draw a line along the edge of a selection. This can help you highlight objects in your image.

Stroke a Selection

1 Select an area of the image with a selection tool.

Note: See Chapter 4 for more about using the selection tools.

2 Click **Edit**.

3 Click **Stroke**.

The Stroke dialog box appears.

4 Type a width in pixels.

5 Select **Inside** to stroke a line on the inside of the selection, **Center** to stroke a line straddling the selection, or **Outside** to stroke a line on the outside of the selection (⊙ changes to ⊙).

● You can click the color box to define the color of the stroke.

6 Click **OK**.

● Photoshop strokes a line along the selection.

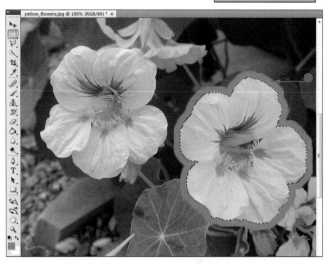

You can select other areas and stroke them using different settings.

● This stroke was applied to the inside of the selection at 40 percent opacity.

TIPS

How do I add a colored border to my image?
Click **Select** and then **All**. Apply the Stroke command, selecting **Inside** as the location (◎ changes to ◉). Photoshop adds a border to the image.

How do I stroke a line a fixed distance outside of an object?
After selecting the object, you can expand your selection and then stroke the line. To expand a selection, click **Select**, **Modify**, and then **Expand**. For more about making selections, see Chapter 4.

Using the Clone Stamp

You can clean up small flaws or erase elements in your image with the Clone Stamp tool. This tool copies information from one area of an image to another.

For other ways to correct defects in your image, see the sections "Using the Healing Brush" and "Using the Patch Tool."

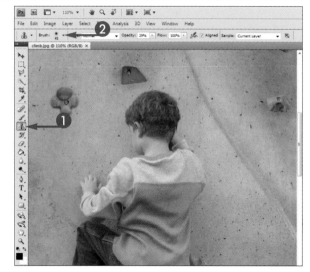

① Click the **Clone Stamp** tool (🖰).

② Click the **Brush** ▾ and select a brush size and type.

③ Press and hold **Alt** (**Option** on a Mac) and click the area of the image from which you want to copy.

● You can specify an opacity of less than 100 percent to apply the tool partially.

You do not need to select an area inside the current image; you can **Alt**+click (**Option**+click on a Mac) another open image.

This example uses the tool to select an empty area of a climbing wall.

④ Release Alt (Option on a Mac).

⑤ Click and drag to apply the Clone Stamp.

Photoshop copies the previously clicked area to where you click and drag.

● As you apply the tool, a preview of the content to be cloned appears inside the brush cursor (◯).

● A ➕ appears at the location from which you are cloning.

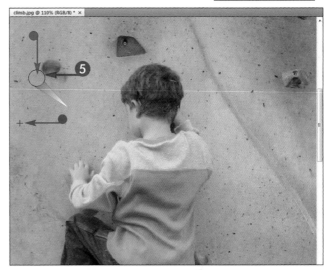

⑥ Click and drag repeatedly over the image to achieve the desired effect.

As you apply the tool, you can press Alt (Option on a Mac) and click again to select a different area from which to copy.

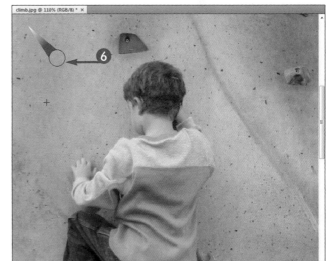

TIP

How can I make the Clone Stamp's effects look seamless?
To erase elements from your image with the Clone Stamp without leaving a trace, try the following:

● Clone between areas of similar color and texture.

● To apply the Clone Stamp more subtly, lower its opacity in the options bar.

● After you click the **Brush** ▾, choose a soft-edged brush shape.

Using the Pattern Stamp

You can paint with a pattern using the Pattern Stamp tool. This tool gives you a free-form way to add repeating elements to your images.

SELECT A PATTERN

1 Click and hold 🖈.

2 From the list that appears, click the **Pattern Stamp** tool (🖈).

3 Click the **Brush** ⸱ and select a brush size and type.

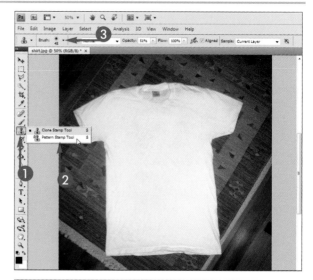

4 Click the **Pattern** ⸱.

5 Select a pattern to apply.

● You can select **Aligned** (☐ changes to ☑) to make your strokes paint the pattern as contiguous tiles.

To create a custom pattern, see the tip on the next page.

6 Click and drag to apply the pattern.

Photoshop applies the pattern wherever you click and drag.

APPLY A DIFFERENT OPACITY

7 Type a value of less than 100 in the Opacity box.

8 Click and drag inside the selection to apply the pattern.

Decreasing the opacity causes the brush to apply a semitransparent pattern.

TIP

How do I define my own custom patterns?

1 Click the **Rectangular Marquee** tool (▢) and select an area in your image.

2 Click **Edit** and **Define Pattern**.

● Your pattern appears in the dialog box.

3 Type a name.

4 Click **OK**.

Using the Healing Brush

You can correct defects in your image using the Healing Brush. The Healing Brush is similar to the Clone Stamp in that it copies pixels from one area of the image to another. However, the Healing Brush takes into account the texture and lighting of the image as it works, which can make its modifications more convincing.

① Click and hold the **Spot Healing Brush** tool ().

② From the list that appears, click the **Healing Brush** tool (🖊).

③ Click the **Brush** ⊡ and specify your brush settings.

● Make sure the **Sampled** option is selected (◯ changes to ◉).

④ Press and hold Alt (Option on a Mac) and click the area of the image you want to heal with.

⑤ Release **Alt** (**Option** on a Mac).

⑥ Click and drag inside the selection to apply the Healing Brush.

Photoshop copies the selected area wherever you click and drag.

⑦ Stop dragging and release the mouse button.

Photoshop adjusts the copied pixels to account for the lighting and texture present in the image.

TIP

How does the Spot Healing Brush tool work?
The Spot Healing Brush is a less interactive version of the Healing Brush. With the Brush settings, you specify the diameter of the area that you want to select. When you click an imperfection in your image, Photoshop attempts to automatically heal the selected area. It replaces the imperfection inside the selected area with the surrounding colors. If you click **Create Texture** (◯ changes to ◉), the tool attempts to mimic the texture of the selected area as well.

The Patch tool enables you to correct defects in your image by selecting them and dragging the selection to an unflawed area of the image. This can be useful if a large part of your image is free of flaws.

For other ways to correct defects in your image, see the sections "Using the Clone Stamp" and "Using the Healing Brush."

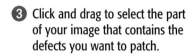

① Click the **Spot Healing Brush** tool (🖊).

② From the list that appears, click the **Patch** tool (◯).

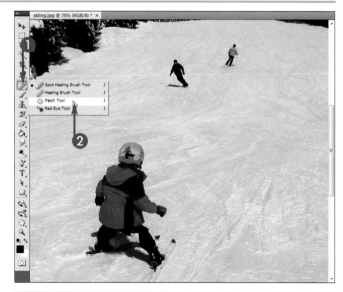

③ Click and drag to select the part of your image that contains the defects you want to patch.

When you make selections, the Patch tool works similarly to the Lasso tool.

Note: *See Chapter 4 for more about the Lasso tool.*

④ Click inside the selection and drag it to an area that does not have defects.

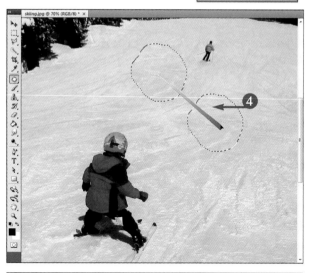

Photoshop uses pixels from the destination selection to patch the defects in the source selection.

● You can select **Destination** (◎ changes to ◉) to patch defects in the reverse order — flaws in the destination selection are corrected with the pixels from the source selection.

TIPS

How does the Patch tool determine what are defects in my selection?

It does this by comparing the colors and textures in the two selections. The tool then tries to eliminate the differences — the defects — while retaining the overall color and texture.

Can I use other selection tools to create my patch selection?

Yes. You can use selection tools such as the Marquee tools and the Lasso tools to define the area you want to patch. Then you can click 🔲 and click and drag the selection to complete the patch.

Using the History Brush

You can use the History brush to paint a previous state of your image from the History panel into the current image. This can be useful if you want to revert just a part of your image.

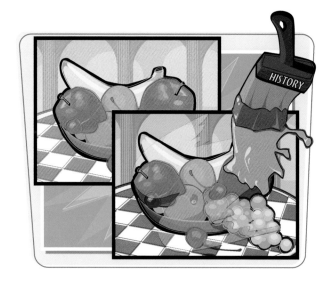

Using the History Brush

PAINT A PREVIOUS STATE

1 Click **Window**.

2 Click **History**.

The History panel opens.

3 Click the **Create New Snapshot** button (🖳) in the History panel.

● Photoshop puts a copy of the current state of the image into the History panel.

4 Modify your image to make it different from the newly created snapshot.

In this example, the Fresco filter was applied and the hue adjusted.

5 Click to the left of the snapshot to select it as the History brush source.

6 Click the **History** brush (🖌).

7 Click the **Brush** ▾ and specify your brush settings.

8 Click and drag inside the image.

Pixels from the previous snapshot are painted into the image.

USING THE ART HISTORY BRUSH

1 Click 🖌.

2 From the list that appears, click the **Art History Brush** tool (🖌).

With the Art History brush, you can paint in snapshot information with an added impressionistic effect.

3 Click the **Brush** ▾ to specify the settings for the brush.

4 Click and drag to apply an artistic effect.

TIP

How do I paint onto a blank image with the History brush?

Start with a photographic image, take a snapshot of it with the **Create New Snapshot** button (📷), and then fill the image with a solid color. See the section "Fill a Selection" for details. You can then use the **History** brush (🖌) to paint in the photographic content.

Using the Eraser

You can delete elements from your images using the Eraser tool. This can be useful when you are trying to separate elements from their backgrounds.

IN THE BACKGROUND LAYER

① Click the Background layer in the Layers panel.

   If you start with a newly scanned image, the Background layer is the only layer.

Note: *See Chapter 8 for more about layers.*

② Click [eraser icon].

③ Click the **Brush** ⊡ and select a brush size and type.

④ Click and drag inside the image.

● Photoshop erases the image by painting with the background color.

IN A REGULAR LAYER

① Click a layer other than the Background layer in the Layers panel.

Note: See Chapter 8 for more about layers.

② Click .

③ Click the **Brush** ⋁ and select a brush size and type.

④ Click and drag inside the image.

Photoshop erases elements in the layer by making pixels transparent.

TIP

How can I quickly erase areas of similar color in my image?

If you click and hold 🖉 in the toolbox, a list appears, and you can select the **Background Eraser** (🖉) or the **Magic Eraser** (🖉). The Background Eraser works by sampling the pixel color beneath the center of the brush and erasing similar colors that are underneath the brush. The Magic Eraser also samples the color beneath the cursor but erases similar pixels throughout the layer. You can adjust the tolerance of both tools in the options bar to control how much they erase.

You can replace colors in your image with the current foreground color using the Color Replacement tool. This gives you a free-form way of recoloring objects in your image, while keeping the shading on the objects intact.

① Click and hold ✏️.

② From the list that appears, click the **Color Replacement** tool (✏️).

③ Click the **Foreground Color** box to select a color for painting.

Note: For details, see the section "Select the Foreground and Background Colors."

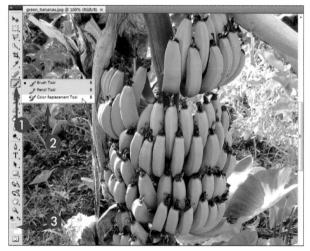

④ Click the **Brush** 🔽 and select a brush size and type.

⑤ Click the **Sampling: Continuous** icon (🖌️).

Sampling: Continuous samples different colors to replace as you paint.

● Sampling: Once (🖌️) samples only the first color you click.

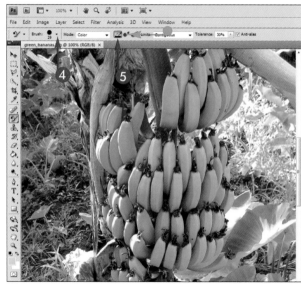

6 Type a tolerance from 1% to 100%.

The greater the tolerance, the greater the range of colors the tool replaces.

7 Click and drag in your image to replace color.

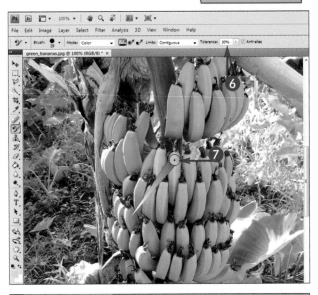

8 Continue to click and drag in your image.

Photoshop replaces more color.

TIP

How does the Color Replacement tool decide what colors to replace?

When you click inside your image, the Color Replacement tool (🖌️) samples the color beneath the cross symbol at the center of the cursor. It then replaces any colors inside the brush that are similar to the sampled color. Photoshop determines similarity based on the Tolerance setting of the tool.

Fix Red Eye in a Photo

You can fix the red-eye effect that occurs in pictures taken with flash in low light by using the Red Eye tool. When applied to the eye of your subject, the tool replaces the reddish pixels in the area with pixels of a predefined color.

Fix Red Eye in a Photo

① Click and hold 📷.

② From the list that appears, click the **Red Eye** tool (📷).

③ Type a value from 1% to 100% for Pupil Size to determine the size of the area affected.

④ Type a value from 1% to 100% for Darken Amount to determine the darkness of the applied color.

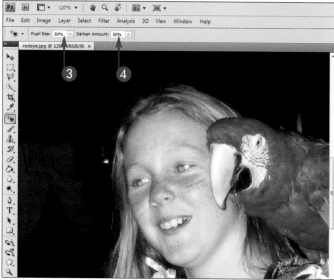

⑤ Click the center of a pupil.

Photoshop replaces the red pixels with a dark-gray hue.

⑥ Click the other eye.

Photoshop fixes the other eye.

TIPS

What are alternatives to the Red Eye tool?

You can use the Color Replacement tool to fix red eye. First, select the red eye with the **Elliptical Marquee** tool (⬭). Select a dark-gray hue as your foreground color, and then apply the foreground color over the eye with the **Color Replacement** tool (🖌). This can also help you fix the blue- and green-eye phenomena that can occur with animals. For more on the Elliptical Marquee tool, see Chapter 4. For more on selecting a foreground color, see the section "Select the Foreground and Background Colors." For more on using the Color Replacement tool, see the section "Replace a Color."

What can cause problems for the Red Eye tool?

If your subject has a reddish skin tone in the photo, the Red Eye tool may apply color to more than just the eyes. To avoid this, you can first select the eyes with the **Elliptical Marquee** tool (⬭). Then the Red Eye tool leaves the rest of the image alone when you apply it. See Chapter 4 for more information.

CHAPTER 7

Adjusting Colors

You can fine-tune the colors in your image — darken them, lighten them, or remove them completely. This chapter introduces the tools that do the trick.

Change Brightness and Contrast

The Brightness/Contrast command provides a simple way to adjust the highlights and shadows in your image.

To change the brightness or contrast of small parts of your image, use the Dodge or Burn tool. See the section "Using the Dodge and Burn Tools" for details.

If you make a selection before using the Brightness/Contrast command, changes affect only the selected pixels. Similarly, if you have a multilayered image, your adjustments affect only the selected layer. See Chapter 4 to make a selection, and Chapter 8 for more about layers.

Change Brightness and Contrast

1 Click **Image**.

2 Click **Adjustments**.

3 Click **Brightness/Contrast**.

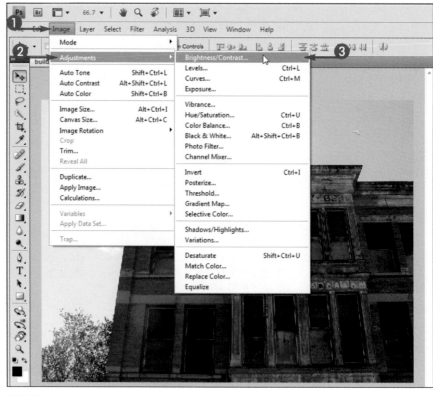

The Brightness/Contrast dialog box appears with sliders set to 0.

4 To display your adjustments in the image window as you make them, select the **Preview** option (☐ changes to ☑).

5 Click and drag the **Brightness** slider (△).

Drag △ to the right to lighten the image, or to the left to darken the image.

● You can also lighten the image by typing a number from 1 to 100, or darken the image by typing a negative number from −1 to −100.

6 Click and drag the **Contrast**
slider (△).

Drag △ to the right to increase
the contrast, or to the left to
decrease the contrast.

Note: *Increasing contrast can bring out details in
your image; decreasing it can soften details.*

● You can also increase the contrast
by typing a number from 1 to
100, or decrease the contrast by
typing a negative number from
−1 to −100.

7 Click **OK**.

Photoshop applies the new
brightness and contrast values.

Note: *You can also apply brightness and contrast
adjustments to an image with an adjustment layer.
See Chapter 8 for more information.*

How can I adjust the contrast of an image automatically?

Click **Image** and then **Auto Contrast**. This converts the lightest
pixels in the image to white and the darkest pixels in the image
to black. Making the highlights brighter and the shadows darker
boosts the contrast, which can improve the appearance of poorly
exposed photographs. In this example, you can use the Auto
Contrast command to bring out the colors in a coastal scene.

Using the Dodge and Burn Tools

You can use the Dodge and Burn tools to brighten or darken specific areas of an image, respectively.

Dodge is a photographic term that describes the diffusing of light when developing a film negative. *Burn* is a photographic term that describes the focusing of light when developing a film negative.

These tools are an alternative to the Brightness/Contrast command, which affects the entire image. To brighten or darken the entire image, see the section "Change Brightness and Contrast."

Using the Dodge and Burn Tools

USING THE DODGE TOOL

1 Click the **Dodge** tool (🔦).

2 Click the **Brush** ⏷.

3 Click the brush you want to use.

● You can also select the range of colors you want to affect and the tool's exposure or strength.

4 Click and drag over the area that you want to lighten.

Photoshop lightens the area.

USING THE BURN TOOL

1. Click and hold .

2. Click the **Burn** tool (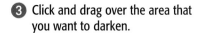) in the list that appears.

● You can select the brush, the range of colors you want to affect, and the tool's exposure, or strength.

3. Click and drag over the area that you want to darken.

Photoshop darkens the area.

TIPS

How do I invert the bright and dark colors in an image?

Click **Image**, **Adjustments**, and then **Invert**. This makes the image look like a film negative. Bright colors become dark, and vice versa.

How can I add extra shadows to the bottom of an object?

Applying the Burn tool () with the Range set to Shadows offers a useful way to add shadows to the shaded side of an object. Likewise, you can use the Dodge tool () with the Range set to Highlights to add highlights to the lighter side of an object.

Using the Blur and Sharpen Tools

You can sharpen or blur specific areas of your image with the Sharpen and Blur tools. This enables you to emphasize or deemphasize objects in a photo.

You can blur or sharpen the entire image by using one of the Blur or Sharpen commands located in Photoshop's Filter menu. See Chapter 10 for more information.

Using the Blur and Sharpen Tools

USING THE BLUR TOOL

1 Click the **Blur** tool ().

2 Click the **Brush** ⏷.

3 Select the brush you want to use.

● To change the strength of the tool, type a value from 1% to 100%.

4 Click and drag an area of the image.

Photoshop blurs the area you click and drag over.

USING THE SHARPEN TOOL

1 Click and hold 🖌️.

2 Click the **Sharpen** tool (🔺) in the list that appears.

● You can type a value from 1% to 100% to set the strength of the tool.

3 Click and drag an area of the image.

Photoshop sharpens the area of the image you click and drag over.

TIP

How do I use the Smudge tool?

The Smudge tool (👆) simulates dragging a finger through wet paint, shifting colors and blurring your image.

1 Click and hold 🖌️.

2 Click 👆.

You can adjust the tool's brush size and strength in the options bar.

3 Click and drag over an area of your image to smudge it.

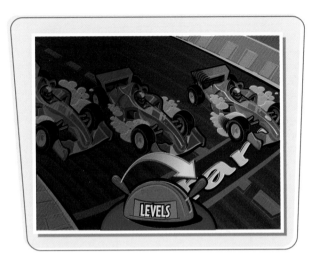

You can use the Levels command to make fine adjustments to the highlights, midtones, or shadows in an image.

Although more difficult to use, the Levels command offers more control over brightness than the Brightness/Contrast command, covered in the section "Change Brightness and Contrast."

To change only selected pixels, select them before performing the Levels command. Similarly, in a multilayered image, your adjustments affect only the selected layer.

Adjust Levels

1 Click **Image**.

2 Click **Adjustments**.

3 Click **Levels**.

The Levels dialog box appears.

4 To display your adjustments in the image window as you make them, select the **Preview** option (☐ changes to ☑).

You can use the Input sliders to adjust an image's brightness, midtones, and highlights.

5 Click and drag ▲ to the right to darken shadows and increase contrast.

6 Click and drag △ to the left to lighten the bright areas of the image and increase contrast.

7 Click and drag ▲ to adjust the midtones of the image.

You can use the Output sliders to decrease the contrast while either lightening or darkening the image.

⑧ Click and drag ▲ to the right to lighten the image.

⑨ Click and drag △ to the left to darken the image.

⑩ Click **OK**.

Photoshop makes brightness and contrast adjustments to the image.

Note: You can also apply levels adjustments to an image with an adjustment layer. See Chapter 8 for more information.

How do I adjust the brightness levels of an image automatically?

Click **Image** and then **Auto Tone**. This converts the lightest pixels in the image to white and the darkest pixels in the image to black. This command is similar to the Auto Contrast command and can quickly improve the contrast of an overly gray photographic image. In this example, the Auto Tone command makes the colors in the barn photo crisper.

Adjust Hue and Saturation

You can change the hue to shift the component colors of an image. You can change the saturation to adjust the color intensity in an image.

If you make a selection before performing the Hue/Saturation command, only the selected pixels are affected. Similarly, if you have a multilayered image, your adjustments affect only the selected layer. See Chapter 4 to make a selection, and Chapter 8 for more about layers.

SATURATION

Adjust Hue and Saturation

1 Click **Image**.

2 Click **Adjustments**.

3 Click **Hue/Saturation**.

The Hue/Saturation dialog box appears.

4 To display your adjustments in the image window as you make them, select the **Preview** option (changes to).

5 Click and drag the **Hue** slider ( ) to shift the colors in the image.

Dragging left or right shifts the colors in different, and sometimes bizarre, ways.

6 Click and drag the **Saturation** slider ( ).

Dragging △ to the right or to the left increases or decreases the intensity of the image's colors, respectively.

● Selecting the **Colorize** option (changes to ✓) partially desaturates the image and adds a single color. You can adjust the color with the sliders.

7 Click **OK**.

Photoshop makes the color adjustments to the image.

Note: You can also apply hue and saturation adjustments to an image with an adjustment layer. See Chapter 8 for more information.

TIPS

How does Photoshop adjust an image's hues?

When you adjust an image's hues in Photoshop, its colors shift according to their position on the color wheel. The color wheel is a graphical way of presenting all the colors in the visible spectrum. Making a positive adjustment with the Hue slider shifts the colors in a counterclockwise direction; making a negative adjustment shifts the colors in a clockwise direction.

How can the Hue/Saturation command enhance my digital photos?

Boosting the saturation can improve photos whose colors appear faded or washed out. Increasing the saturation by 10 to 20 points is often enough to enhance the colors without making them look artificially bright.

Using the Sponge Tool

You can use the Sponge tool to adjust the color saturation, or color intensity, of a specific area of an image. This can help bring out the colors in washed-out areas of photos, or mute colors in areas that are too bright.

Using the Sponge Tool

DECREASE SATURATION

① Click and hold ✎.

② Click the **Sponge** tool (🟤) in the list that appears.

③ Click the **Brush** ⏷ and select the brush you want to use.

④ Click here and select **Desaturate**.

⑤ Click and drag the mouse (◯) to decrease the saturation of an area of the image.

INCREASE SATURATION

1. Perform Steps **1** to **3** on the previous page.

2. Click here and select **Saturate**.

3. Click and drag ◯ over an area of the image.

Photoshop increases the saturation of that area of the image.

● You can adjust the strength of the Sponge tool by typing a new Flow setting from 1% to 100%.

TIP

How can I easily convert a color image to a grayscale image?

1. Click **Image**.
2. Click **Adjustments**.
3. Click **Desaturate**.

● Photoshop sets the saturation value of the image to 0, effectively converting it to a grayscale image.

Note: For more control over your conversion, see "Convert to Black and White."

Adjust Color Balance

You can use the Color Balance command to change the amounts of specific colors in your image. This can be useful if you need to remove a colorcast introduced by a scanner or by age.

If you make a selection before performing the Color Balance command, only the selected pixels are affected. Similarly, if you have a multilayered image, your adjustments affect only the selected layer. See Chapter 4 to make a selection and Chapter 8 for more about layers.

Adjust Color Balance

1 Click **Image**.

2 Click **Adjustments**.

3 Click **Color Balance**.

The Color Balance dialog box appears.

4 To display your adjustments in the image window as you make them, select the **Preview** option (☐ changes to ☑).

5 Select the tones in the image that you want to affect (◎ changes to ◉).

6 Click and drag a color slider (△) toward the color you want to add more of.

To add a warm cast to your image, you can drag a slider toward red or magenta.

To add a cool cast, you can drag a slider toward blue or cyan.

7 Select another Tone Balance option.

8 Type a number from –100 to 100 in one or more of the Color Levels fields.

Note: Step 8 is an alternative to dragging a slider.

9 Click **OK**.

Photoshop makes color adjustments to the image.

Note: You can also apply color balance adjustments to an image with an adjustment layer. See Chapter 8 for more information.

 TIPS

How can the Color Balance command help me improve poorly lit digital photos?

The Color Balance command can help eliminate the colorcast that can sometimes permeate a digital photo. For example, some indoor incandescent or fluorescent lighting can add a yellowish or bluish tint to your images. You can remove these tints by adding blue or red, respectively, to your images using this command.

How can I convert my image to black and white pixels?

Click **Image**, **Adjustments**, and **Threshold**. A Bitmap dialog box appears, enabling you to choose a method for converting the pixels. This command makes your image look like a photocopy.

Using the Variations Command

The Variations command includes a user-friendly interface that enables you to adjust the color in your image.

If you make a selection before performing the Variations command, only the selected pixels are affected. Similarly, if you have a multilayered image, your adjustments affect only the selected layer. See Chapter 4 to make a selection, and Chapter 8 for more about layers.

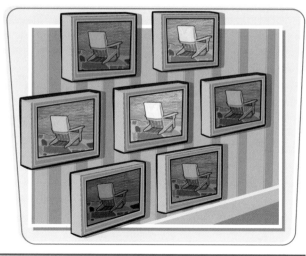

Using the Variations Command

1 Click **Image**.

2 Click **Adjustments**.

3 Click **Variations**.

4 In the Variations dialog box, select a tonal range of your image to adjust (◎ changes to ●).

● Alternatively, you can select **Saturation**, or strength of color (◎ changes to ●).

5 Click and drag △ left to perform small adjustments, or right to make large adjustments.

6 To add a color to your image, click one of the **More** thumbnails.

● The result of the adjustment appears in the Current Pick thumbnails.

To increase the effect, you can click the **More** thumbnail again.

● You can increase the brightness of the image by clicking **Lighter**.

● You can decrease the brightness by clicking **Darker**.

7 Click **OK**.

Photoshop makes the color adjustments to the image.

In this example, some of the blue colorcast is replaced with yellow.

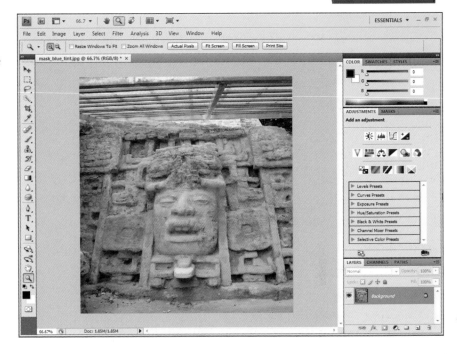

TIP

How can I undo color adjustments while using the Variations dialog box?

If you clicked one of the **More** thumbnail images to increase a color, you can click the **More** thumbnail image opposite to undo the effect.

When you add colors in equal amounts to an image, the colors opposite one another — for example, Green (●) and Magenta (●) — cancel each other out.

Note that clicking the Original image in the upper left corner returns the image to its original state as well.

Match Colors between Images

You can use the Match Color command to match the colors in one image with the colors from another. For example, you can apply the colors from a bluish shoreline image to a reddish desert image to give the desert image a cooler appearance.

① Open a source image from which you want to match colors.

② Open a destination image whose colors you want to change.

Make sure the image window for the destination image is selected.

③ Click **Image**.

④ Click **Adjustments**.

⑤ Click **Match Color**.

The Match Color dialog box appears.

⑥ Click here and select the file name of the source image.

7 Click and drag the sliders (△) to control how the new colors are applied.

Luminance controls the brightness.

Color Intensity controls the saturation.

Fade controls how much color Photoshop replaces; you can increase the Fade value to greater than 0 to only partially replace the color.

8 Click **OK**.

Photoshop replaces the colors in the destination image with those in the source image.

● In this example, Photoshop applies the vibrant greens and yellows from a banana bunch to a less colorful photo of a child and a wall.

TIP

How do I match colors using colors from only a selected part of my source image?

Make a selection before performing Steps **3** to **5** in this section, and then select the **Use Selection in Source to Calculate Colors** option (○ changes to ●) in the Match Color dialog box. Photoshop uses only colors from inside the selection to determine color replacement.

Correct Shadows and Highlights

You can quickly correct images with overly dark or light areas using the Shadows/Highlights command. This command can help correct photos that have a shadowed subject due to backlighting.

If you make a selection before performing the Shadows/Highlights command, only the selected pixels are affected. Similarly, if you have a multilayered image, your adjustments affect only the selected layer. See Chapter 4 to make a selection, and Chapter 8 for more about layers.

Correct Shadows and Highlights

① Click **Image**.

② Click **Adjustments**.

③ Click **Shadows/Highlights**.

The Shadows/Highlights dialog box appears.

④ Click and drag the **Amount** slider (△) in the Shadows section.

The farther you drag △ to the right, the more the shadows lighten.

● You can also adjust the shadows by typing a number from 0 to 100.

⑤ Click and drag the **Amount** slider
(△) in the Highlights section.

The farther you drag △ to the
right, the more the highlights
darken.

● You can also adjust the highlights
by typing a number from 0 to 100.

⑥ Click **OK**.

Photoshop adjusts the shadows
and highlights in the image.

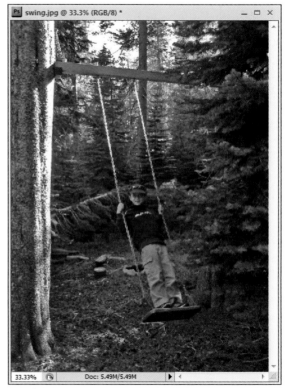

TIP

**How do I get more control over how the Shadows/Highlights
command affects my shadows and highlights?**

Select **Show More Options** (☐ changes to ☑) in the Shadows/Highlights
dialog box. Additional settings appear. Adjusting the Tonal Width sliders
helps you control what parts of the image are considered shadows and
highlights. The Radius sliders help you control the contrast in the adjusted
shadows and highlights.

Create a Duotone

You can convert a grayscale image to a duotone. This is an easy way to add some color to a black-and-white photo.

A *duotone* is essentially a grayscale image with a color tint.

Create a Duotone

① Click **Image**.

② Click **Mode**.

③ Click **Grayscale**.

④ In the message box that appears, click **Discard**.

Photoshop converts your image to grayscale.

⑤ Click **Image**.

⑥ Click **Mode**.

⑦ Click **Duotone**.

The Duotone Options dialog box opens.

⑧ Click here and select **Duotone**.

9 Click the first color swatch.

The Select ink color dialog box opens.

10 Click inside the window to select your first duotone color.

● You can click and drag the slider () to change the color selection.

11 Click **OK**.

12 Type a name for the color.

13 Click the second color swatch.

The Color Libraries dialog box appears.

14 Click inside the window to select your second duotone color.

15 Click **OK** in the Color Libraries dialog box.

16 Click **OK** in the Duotone Options dialog box.

Photoshop uses the two selected colors to create the tones in the image.

TIPS

How can I use duotones to enliven a project?
Duotones offer a quick and easy way to add color to a Web page or printed publication when all you have available are grayscale images.

Can I combine more than two colors to create the tones in my grayscale image?
Yes. You can combine three colors to create a tritone or four colors to create a quadtone. Select **Tritone** or **Quadtone** in Step 8 to create these types of images. You can also select **Monotone** to create your image tones using a single color.

Convert to Black and White

You can use the Black and White interface to remove colors in a photo, and then adjust various sliders to control the lightness and darkness of the different areas of the photo.

If you make a selection before performing the Black and White command, only the selected pixels are affected. Similarly, if you have a multilayered image, your adjustments affect only the selected layer. See Chapter 4 to make a selection, and Chapter 8 for more about layers.

ADJUST LIGHTING WITH SLIDERS

① Click **Image**.

② Click **Adjustments**.

③ Click **Black & White**.

The Black and White dialog box appears.

Photoshop converts your image to grayscale.

④ Click and drag a color slider (△) to adjust the lightness of a color in the image.

The sliders correspond to the colors in the original image.

Drag the slider to the left to darken a color.

Drag the slider to the right to lighten a color.

Photoshop adjusts the color.

● In this example, the sky is darkened by clicking and dragging the **Cyans** slider to the left.

⑤ Click **OK** to apply the adjustment.

ADJUST LIGHTING WITH THE MOUSE

① With the Black and White dialog box open, click inside the image and hold down the mouse button (⟨ᐟ⟩ changes to ⟨🖉⟩).

● Photoshop reads the clicked color and highlights the relevant color in the dialog box.

② With the mouse button down, drag the cursor to the left or right to adjust the color lightness (⟨🖉⟩ changes to ⟨🖑⟩).

③ Click **OK** to apply the adjustment.

How can I tint my image using the Black and White tool?

① In the Black and White dialog box, click **Tint** (☐ changes to ☑).

Photoshop tints the image.

② Click and drag the **Hue** slider (△) to control the color of the tint.

● You can also click the color box to select a tint color.

③ Click and drag the **Saturation** slider (△) to control the intensity of the tint.

④ Click **OK** to apply the adjustment.

Adjust Vibrance

The Vibrance command can boost the intensity of the colors in an image, helping you improve the look of a faded or washed-out photo. You can also use the command to mute an overly colorful image.

If you make a selection before performing the Vibrance command, only the selected pixels are affected. Similarly, if you have a multilayered image, your adjustments affect only the selected layer. See Chapter 4 to make a selection, and Chapter 8 for more about layers.

Adjust Vibrance

① Click **Image**.

② Click **Adjustments**.

③ Click **Vibrance**.

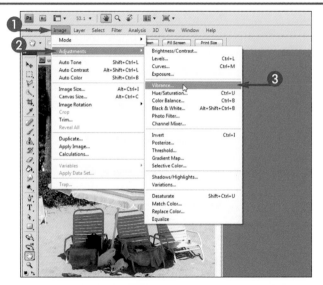

The Vibrance dialog box appears.

④ To display your adjustments in the image window as you make them, select the **Preview** option (☐ changes to ☑).

⑤ Click and drag the **Vibrance** slider (△) to adjust the intensity of the colors.

The Vibrance setting takes into account the current saturation of the colors, emphasizing colors that are less intense.

⑥ Click and drag the **Saturation** slider (△) to adjust the intensity of the colors in the image.

The Saturation setting changes the intensity evenly across all colors.

⑦ Click **OK**.

Photoshop applies the
adjustment.

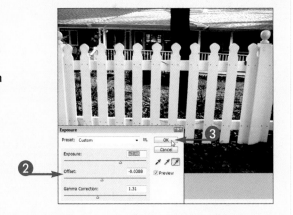

TIP

How can I improve an under- or over-exposed image?

You can fix exposure problems using the Exposure
command.

① Click **Image**, **Adjustments**, and then **Exposure** to open
the Exposure dialog box.

② Make exposure adjustments by dragging the
sliders (△).

You can drag the **Exposure** slider to adjust
highlights.

You can drag the **Offset** slider to adjust shadows
and midtones.

You can drag the **Gamma** slider to adjust the
gamma brightness function, which can correct for
varying monitor brightnesses.

③ Click **OK** to apply the adjustment.

Note: To locally adjust exposure, see "Using the Dodge and Burn Tools."

Working with Layers

You can separate the elements in your image so that you can move and transform them independently of one another. You can accomplish this by placing them in different layers.

What Are Layers?

A Photoshop image can consist of multiple layers, with each layer containing different objects in the image.

When you open a digital-camera photo or a newly scanned image in Photoshop, it exists as a single layer known as the Background layer. You can add new layers on top of the Background layer as you work.

Layer Independence

Layered Photoshop files act like several images combined into one. Each layer of an image has its own set of pixels that you can move and transform independently of the pixels in other layers.

Apply Commands to Layers

Most Photoshop commands affect only the layer that you select. For example, if you click and drag using the Move tool (), the selected layer moves while the other layers stay in place. If you apply a color adjustment, only colors in the selected layer change.

Manipulate Layers

You can combine, duplicate, and hide layers in an image, and shuffle their order. You can also link particular layers so that they move in unison, or blend content from different layers in creative ways. You manage all this in Photoshop's Layers panel.

Transparency

Layers can have transparent areas, where the elements in the layers below can show through. When you perform a cut or erase command on a layer, the affected pixels become transparent. You can also make a layer partially transparent by decreasing its opacity or its fill.

Adjustment Layers

Adjustment layers are special layers that contain information about color or tonal adjustments. An adjustment layer affects the pixels in all the layers below it. You can increase or decrease an adjustment layer's intensity to get precisely the effect you want.

Save Layered Files

You can save multilayered images only in the Photoshop, PDF, and TIFF file formats. To save a layered image in another file format — for example, BMP, GIF, or JPEG — you must combine the image's layers into a single layer, a process known as *flattening*. For more information about saving files, see Chapter 14.

Create and Add to a Layer

To keep elements in your image independent of one another, you can create separate layers and add objects to them.

CREATE A LAYER

① Click the **Layers** tab to select the Layers panel.

If the Layers tab is hidden, you can click **Window** and then **Layers** to open the Layers panel.

② Click the layer above which you want to add the new layer.

③ In the Layers panel, click the **New Layer** button (🔲).

Alternatively, you can click **Layer**, **New**, and then **Layer**.

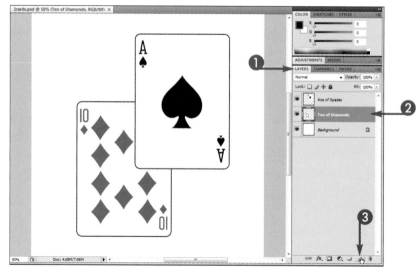

● Photoshop creates a new, transparent layer.

Note: To change the name of a layer, see the section "Rename a Layer."

COPY AND PASTE INTO A LAYER

Note: *This example shows how to add content to the new layer by copying and pasting from another image file.*

1 Open another image.

2 Using a selection tool, select the content you want to copy into the other image.

Note: *See Chapter 1 for more about opening an image; see Chapter 4 for more about the selection tools.*

3 Click **Edit**.

4 Click **Copy**.

View the image where you created the new layer.

5 Click the new layer in the Layers panel.

6 Click **Edit**.

7 Click **Paste**.

● The selected content from the other image appears in the new layer.

TIPS

What is the Background layer?

The Background layer is the default bottom layer that appears when you create a new image that has a nontransparent background color, or when you import an image from a scanner or digital camera. You can create new layers on top of a Background layer but not below it. Unlike other layers, a Background layer cannot contain transparent pixels.

How can I copy layers between images?

If you have multiple images open in Photoshop, you can click and drag a layer from the Layers panel of one image into the window of a different image. Photoshop copies the layer into the second image. You can move multiple layers by Ctrl +clicking (⌘+clicking) them and then dragging them to a different image window.

Hide
a Layer

Hide
a Layer

You can hide a layer to temporarily remove elements in that layer from view.

Hidden layers do not appear when you print or use the Save for Web command.

Hide a Layer

1 Click the **Layers** tab to select the Layers panel.

If the Layers tab is hidden, you can click **Window** and then **Layers** to open the Layers panel.

2 Click the visibility icon (👁) for a layer.

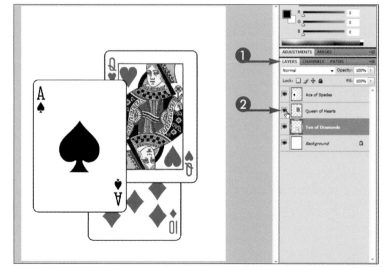

● The icon disappears.

Photoshop hides the layer.

To show one layer and hide all the others, you can press Alt (Option on a Mac) and click 👁 for the layer you want to show. Pressing Alt (Option on a Mac) and clicking again makes the other layers reappear.

Note: *You can also delete a layer. See the section "Delete a Layer" for more information.*

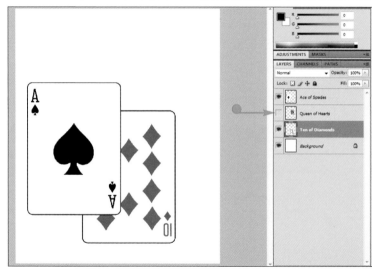

Move a Layer

You can use the Move tool to reposition the elements in one layer without moving those in others.

Move a Layer

1 Click the **Layers** tab to select the Layers panel.

If the Layers tab is hidden, you can click **Window** and then **Layers** to open the panel.

2 Click a layer.

3 Click the **Move** tool (⊕).

4 Click and drag inside the window.

Content in the selected layer moves.

Content in the other layers does not move.

Note: To move several layers at the same time, see the section "Link Layers."

Duplicate a Layer

By duplicating a layer, you can manipulate elements in an image while keeping a copy of their original state.

Duplicate a Layer

① Click the **Layers** tab to select the Layers panel.

If the Layers tab is hidden, you can click **Window** and then **Layers** to open the Layers panel.

② Click a layer.

③ Click and drag the layer to ▣.

Alternatively, you can click **Layer** and then **Duplicate Layer**; a dialog box appears, asking you to name the duplicate layer.

● Photoshop duplicates the selected layer.

Note: To rename the duplicate layer, see the section "Rename a Layer."

● You can see that Photoshop has duplicated the layer by selecting the new layer, clicking 🔁, and clicking and dragging the layer.

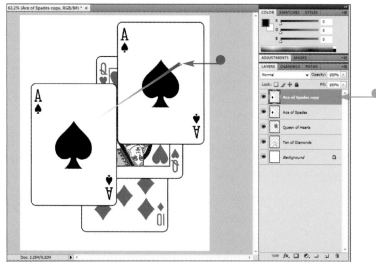

Delete a Layer

You can delete a layer when you no longer have a use for its contents.

Delete a Layer

1. Click the **Layers** tab to select the Layers panel.

2. Click a layer.

3. Click and drag the layer to the trash icon ( ).

   Alternatively, you can click **Layer** and then **Delete Layer**, or you can select a layer and click . In both cases, a confirmation dialog box appears.

Photoshop deletes the selected layer, and the content in the layer disappears from the image window.

Note: You can also hide a layer. See the section "Hide a Layer" for more information.

Reorder Layers

You can change the stacking order of layers to move elements forward or backward in your image.

USING THE LAYERS PANEL

1. Click the **Layers** tab to select the Layers panel.

   If the Layers tab is hidden, you can click **Window** and then **Layers** to open the panel.

2. Click a layer other than the Background layer.

3. Click and drag the layer to change its position in the stack.

● The layer assumes its new position in the stack.

USING THE ARRANGE COMMANDS

1. In the Layers panel, click a layer other than the Background layer.

2. Click **Layer**.

3. Click **Arrange**.

4. Click the command for how you want to move the layer.

   You can select **Bring to Front**, **Bring Forward**, **Send Backward**, **Send to Back**, or **Reverse**.

   In this example, Bring Forward is selected.

● The layer assumes its new position in the stack.

Note: You cannot move a layer below the default Background layer.

Are there shortcuts for changing the order of layers?

You can shift layers forward and backward in the stack by pressing the following shortcuts keys:

Move ...	Windows Shortcut	Mac Shortcut
... forward one step	Ctrl +]	⌘ +]
... backward one step	Ctrl + [	⌘ + [
... to the very front	Shift + Ctrl +]	Shift + ⌘ +]
... to the very back	Shift + Ctrl + [	Shift + ⌘ + [

Change the Opacity of a Layer

Adjusting the opacity of a layer can let elements in the layers below show through. *Opacity* is the opposite of transparency. Decreasing the opacity of a layer increases its transparency.

Change the Opacity of a Layer

① Click the **Layers** tab to select the Layers panel.

If the Layers tab is hidden, you can click **Window** and then **Layers** to open the Layers panel.

② Click a layer other than the Background layer.

Note: *You cannot change the opacity of the Background layer.*

● The default opacity is 100 percent, which is completely opaque.

③ Type a new value in the Opacity field and press Enter (Return on a Mac).

● Alternatively, you can click ▸ and drag the slider.

A layer's opacity can range from 0 to 100 percent.

● The layer changes in opacity.

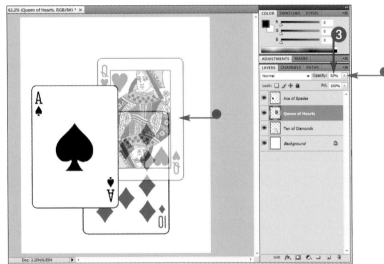

A shortcut for changing a layer's opacity is to click the layer and press a number key.

● In this example, 3 is pressed, which changes the opacity to 30 percent.

You can make multiple layers in your image semitransparent by changing their opacities.

● In this example, both the Queen of Hearts and Ten of Diamonds layers are semitransparent.

What is the Fill setting in the Layers panel?

It is similar to the Opacity setting, except that lowering it does not affect any blending options or layer styles applied to the layer. For example, if you apply a drop shadow to a layer, lowering the Fill setting makes the layer object more transparent but does not affect the shadow behind the object. Lowering the Opacity setting does affect blending options and layer styles. For more about blending options, see the section "Blend Layers." For more about layer styles, see Chapter 9.

Merge and Flatten Layers

Merging layers enables you to permanently combine information from two or more separate layers. Flattening layers combines all the layers of an image into one.

MERGE LAYERS

1. Click the **Layers** tab to select the Layers panel.

2. Click a layer to select it.

3. While pressing Ctrl (⌘ on a Mac), click one or more layers to merge with the selected layer.

4. Click **Layer**.

5. Click **Merge Layers**.

● The layers merge.

Photoshop keeps the name of the uppermost layer. The merged layers also assume the position of the uppermost layer.

● To see the result of the merge, select the new layer, click ⊕, and click and drag the merged layer; the elements that were previously in separate layers now move together.

FLATTEN LAYERS

① Click **Layer**.

② Click **Flatten Image**.

● All the layers merge into one background layer.

● You can also access Merge and Flatten commands in the Layers panel menu. Click ▤ to access them.

TIPS

Why would I want to merge layers?

Merging layers enables you to save computer memory. The fewer layers a Photoshop image has, the less space it takes up in RAM and on your hard drive when you save it. Merging layers also lets you permanently combine elements of your image when you are happy with how you have arranged them relative to one another. If you want the option of rearranging all the original layers in the future, save a copy of your image before you merge layers.

What happens to layers when I save an image for the Web?

When creating a JPEG, non-animated GIF, or PNG file for publishing on the Web, Photoshop automatically flattens the layers of an image before creating the new file. Your original Photoshop image retains its layers. For more information about saving images, see Chapter 14.

Rename a Layer

You can rename a layer to give it a name that describes its content. Giving your layers descriptive names can be helpful when you are managing many layers in a single image.

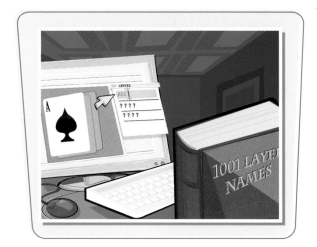

Rename a Layer

① Click the **Layers** tab to select the Layers panel.

If the Layers tab is hidden, you can click **Window** and then **Layers** to open the Layers panel.

② Click a layer.

③ Click **Layer**.

④ Click **Layer Properties**.

The Layer Properties dialog box appears.

⑤ Type a new name for the layer.

⑥ Click **OK**.

● The name of the layer changes in the Layers panel.

You can also double-click the name of the layer in the Layers panel to edit the name in place.

Transform a Layer

You can use a transform tool to change the shape of the objects in a layer. When you transform a layer, the rest of your image remains unchanged.

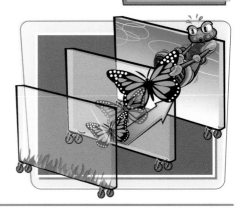

Transform a Layer

1 Click the **Layers** tab to select the Layers panel.

If the Layers tab is hidden, you can click **Window** and then **Layers** to open the Layers panel.

2 Click **Edit**.

3 Click **Transform**.

4 Click a transform command.

You can also click the **Move** tool (⊹) and click **Show Transform Controls** in the options bar.

5 Click and drag the side and corner handles to transform the shape of the layer.

6 Click ✓ or press Enter (⌘+Return on a Mac) to apply the change.

● You can click ⊘ or press Esc to cancel the change.

Photoshop changes your image according to the transform command you select.

Note: For more about transforming your images, see Chapter 5.

Create a Solid Fill Layer

You can create a solid fill layer to place an opaque layer of color throughout your image. You can use fill layers that contrast with the objects in layers above them to make those objects stand out.

1 Click the **Layers** tab to select the Layers panel.

If the Layers tab is hidden, you can click **Window** and then **Layers** to open the Layers panel.

2 Click the layer above which you want to add solid color.

3 Click **Layer**.

4 Click **New Fill Layer**.

5 Click **Solid Color**.

● You can also click the **Create New Fill or Adjustment Layer** button (⬤) and select **Solid Color**.

The New Layer dialog box appears.

6 Type a name for the layer.

● You can specify a blend mode or opacity setting for the layer.

Note: *See the section "Blend Layers" or "Change the Opacity of a Layer" for details.*

7 Click **OK**.

The Color Picker dialog box appears.

⑧ To change the range of colors that appears in the window, click and drag the slider (⊠).

⑨ To select a fill color, click in the color window.

⑩ Click **OK**.

● Photoshop creates a new layer filled with a solid color.

Layers below the new fill layer are covered while the layers above the new layer are not affected.

TIPS

How do I add solid color to just part of a layer?

Make a selection with a selection tool before creating the solid fill layer. Photoshop adds color only inside the selection.

What other types of fill layers can I create?

You can add a gradient fill layer that shows a transition from one color to another by clicking **Layer**, **New Fill Layer**, and then **Gradient**. You can add a pattern fill later that displays a repeated design by clicking **Layer**, **New Fill Layer**, and then **Pattern**.

Create an Adjustment Layer

Adjustment layers let you store color and tonal changes in a layer instead of having them permanently applied to your image. The information in an adjustment layer is applied to the pixels in the layers below it.

You can use adjustment layers to test an editing technique without applying it to the original layer. Adjustment layers are especially handy for experimenting with colors, tones, and brightness settings.

Create an Adjustment Layer

① Click the **Layers** tab to display the Layers panel.

② Click the **Adjustments** tab to display the Adjustments panel.

If a panel tab is not visible, you can click **Window** and then the panel name to display the panel.

③ Click the layer above which you want to create an adjustment layer.

④ Click an adjustment layer button.

Note: *See the tip on the next page for a description of the adjustment types.*

● Photoshop places the new adjustment layer above the selected layer.

● You can specify a blend mode or opacity setting for the layer.

Note: *See the section "Blend Layers" or "Change the Opacity of a Layer" for details.*

● The settings for the adjustment command appear in the Adjustments panel.

5 Click and drag the sliders (△) or type values to adjust the settings.

In this example, an adjustment layer is created that changes the hue and saturation.

Photoshop applies the effect to the layers below the adjustment layer, including the Background layer.

● In this example, the adjustment layer affects the card layers below it while leaving the card layer above it unaffected.

● You can click **Clip to Layer** (⦿) to have the adjustment layer affect only the layer directly below it.

6 Click **Return to Adjustment List** (⬐) to return a list of adjustments in the Adjustments panel.

TIP

What types of adjustments can I apply to my image?

The adjustments are also available as commands, accessible by clicking **Image** and then **Adjustments**. Some of these commands are covered in Chapter 7. For the others, see the Photoshop help documentation.

🔆 Brightness/Contrast	📊 Levels	📈 Curves	✨ Exposure
▽ Vibrance	🎨 Hue/Saturation	🔺 Color Balance	◼ Black & White
🔍 Photo Filter	🔁 Channel Mixer	🔳 Invert	▨ Posterize
▨ Threshold	▬ Gradient Map	🔲 Selective Color	

Edit an Adjustment Layer

You can modify the color and tonal changes that you defined in an adjustment layer. This enables you to fine-tune your adjustment layer to get the effect you want.

You can decrease the opacity of an adjustment layer to lessen its effect on the layers below it.

Edit an Adjustment Layer

1 Click the **Layers** tab to display the Layers panel.

2 Click the **Adjustments** tab to display the Adjustments panel.

You can click **Window** and then the panel name to display a panel if its tab is not visible.

3 Click the adjustment layer that you want to edit.

The settings corresponding to the adjustment command appear in the Adjustments panel.

4 Click and drag △ to change the settings in the panel.

Photoshop applies your changes.

In this example, the hue is changed, which shifts the color in the layers below the adjustment layer.

● You can lessen the effect of an adjustment layer by decreasing the layer's opacity to less than 100 percent.

● In this example, the opacity was decreased to 60 percent, which reverses the decrease in saturation. Some of the original color in the cards returns.

● You can click 🗑 to delete the selected adjustment layer.

How do I merge an adjustment layer with a regular layer?

① Place the adjustment layer above the layer with which you want to merge it.

② Click **Layer** and then **Merge Down**.

Photoshop applies the adjustment layer's effects to the layer below it.

The adjustment layer is removed from the Layers panel.

Apply an Adjustment-Layer Preset

Photoshop offers a variety of
ready-to-use adjustment layers
that apply common color-
correction techniques and special
effects. After you apply them,
you can make changes to their
settings in the Adjustments
panel.

Apply an Adjustment-Layer Preset

1 Click the **Layers** tab to display
the Layers panel.

2 Click the **Adjustments** tab to
display the Adjustments panel.

You can click **Window** and then
the panel name to display a panel
if its tab is not visible.

3 Click the layer above which you
want to create an adjustment
layer.

4 Click ▷ to open a list of
adjustment-layer presets
(▷ changes to ▽).

⑤ Click a preset.

● Photoshop creates a new adjustment layer for the preset.

● The settings appear in the Adjustments panel.

The settings affect the layers below the adjustment layer, including the Background layer.

● You can click ⬤ to have the adjustment layer affect only the layer directly below it.

⑥ Click ◀ to return to a list of adjustments in the Adjustments panel.

How do I save an adjustment layer as a preset?
You can save your own adjustment layers as presets and then apply those layers to future projects.

❶ Create an adjustment layer and select it in the Layers panel.

❷ Click ▤ in the Adjustments panel.

❸ Click **Save Preset**. The command name will differ depending on the type of adjustment layer you are saving.

A Save dialog box appears enabling you to name and save the preset.

After saving, your preset appears in the Adjustments panel preset list.

Link Layers

Linking causes different layers to move in unison when you rearrange them with the Move tool. You may find linking useful when you want to keep elements of an image aligned with one another, but do not want to merge their layers. See the section "Merge and Flatten Layers" for more about merging. Keeping layers unmerged enables you to apply effects independently to each one.

CREATE A LINK

① Click the **Layers** tab to select the Layers panel.

If the Layers tab is hidden, you can click **Window** and then **Layers** to open the Layers panel.

② While pressing Ctrl (⌘ on a Mac), click the layers you want to link.

③ Click **Layer**.

④ Click **Link Layers**.

● Doing so turns on a linking icon (⊖).

The layers link together.

MOVE LINKED LAYERS

① Click the **Move** tool ().

② Click and drag inside the image window.

The linked layers move together.

UNLINK LAYERS

① While pressing Ctrl (⌘ on a Mac), click the layers you want to unlink.

② Click **Layer**.

③ Click **Unlink Layers**.

Photoshop removes the link.

How do I keep from changing a layer after I have it the way I want it?

You can lock the layer by selecting the layer and clicking the **Lock All** icon () in the Layers panel. You cannot move, delete, or otherwise edit a locked layer. You can click the **Lock Transparent Pixels** icon () to prevent a user from editing the transparent pixels in the layer. Clicking the **Lock Image Pixels** icon () locks the nontransparent pixels in a layer, and clicking the **Lock Position** icon () locks the position of a layer.

Blend Layers

You can use Photoshop's blending modes to specify how pixels in a layer should blend with the layers below. You can blend layers to create all kinds of visual effects in your photos.

In the following example, two photos are combined in one image file as two separate layers and then the layers are blended together. To copy a photo into a layer, see the section "Create and Add to a Layer."

Blend Layers

BLEND A REGULAR LAYER

1 Click the **Layers** tab to select the Layers panel.

If the Layers tab is hidden, you can click **Window** and then **Layers** to open the Layers panel.

2 Click the layer that you want to blend.

3 Click here and select a blend mode.

Photoshop blends the selected layer with the layers below it.

This example blends a sunset layer with a layer of a woman by using the Hard Light mode.

BLEND AN ADJUSTMENT LAYER

1. Click the **Layers** tab to select the Layers panel.

   If the Layers tab is hidden, you can click **Window** and then **Layers** to open the Layers panel.

2. Click the adjustment layer that you want to blend.

3. Click here and select a blend mode.

Photoshop blends the selected layer with the layers below it.

This example shows the Exclusion mode applied to a Hue and Saturation adjustment layer, which creates a photonegative effect where the layers overlap.

TIP

What effects do some of the different blending modes have?

- **Multiply**: Darkens the colors where the selected layer overlaps layers below it.
- **Screen**: The opposite of Multiply. It lightens colors where layers overlap.
- **Color**: Takes the selected layer's colors and blends them with the details in the layers below it.
- **Luminosity**: The opposite of Color. It takes the selected layer's details and mixes them with the colors below it.

Work with Smart Objects

You can convert a layer into a Smart Object. Unlike a regular layer, Photoshop remembers the original composition of a Smart Object, so you can resize and perform other operations on it without its quality degrading.

CREATE A SMART OBJECT

1. Click the layer to convert into a Smart Object.

2. Click **Layer**.

3. Click **Smart Objects**.

4. Click **Convert to Smart Object**.

● Photoshop converts the layer to a Smart Object.

Smart Objects are designated with a special icon (⬚) in the Layers panel.

196

DUPLICATE A SMART OBJECT

1. Click a Smart Object in the Layers panel.

2. Click **Layer**.

3. Click **Smart Objects**.

4. Click **New Smart Object via Copy**.

● Photoshop duplicates the Smart Object. The new Smart Object appears in the Layers panel.

5. Click ▶+.

6. Click and drag to view the new Smart Object.

TIP

How do I convert a Smart Object back to a regular layer?

1. Click the Smart Object in the Layers panel.

2. Click **Layer** and then click **Smart Objects**.

3. Click **Rasterize**.

Photoshop converts the Smart Object back to a layer.

continued

197

Work with Smart Objects *(continued)*

Because Photoshop remembers the original composition of a Smart Object, you can transform the object multiple times without it degrading in quality like a normal object would.

SCALE A SMART OBJECT

1. Click to select the Smart Object in the Layers panel.

2. Click **Edit**.

3. Click **Transform**.

4. Click **Scale**.

A rectangular bounding box with handles on the sides and corners surrounds the object.

5. Click and drag the handles to shrink the object.

6. Click ✓ or press Enter
   (⌘ + Return on a Mac)
   to commit the scaling.

● Photoshop shrinks the object.

⑦ Repeat Steps 2 to 4.

⑧ Click and drag the handles to enlarge the object.

⑨ Click ✓ or press Enter (⌘ + Return on a Mac) to commit the scaling.

● Photoshop enlarges the object.

Because Photoshop remembers the pixel information associated with the original object, the quality of the Smart Object is not degraded when you rescale it to its original size.

TIP

How can I insert another image into my project as a Smart Object?

① Click **File** and then click **Place**.

② In the Place dialog box, click the image file.

③ Click **Place**.

④ Press Enter (Return on a Mac) to complete the Place command.

Photoshop adds the image as a Smart Object.

Applying Layer Styles

You can apply special effects to layers using Photoshop's built-in layer styles. With these styles, you can add shadows, glows, and 3-D appearances to your layers. Photoshop's Styles panel enables you to easily apply predefined combinations of styles to your image or create your own.

Apply a Drop Shadow

You can apply a drop shadow to make a layer look as though it is floating above the image canvas.

Apply a Drop Shadow

1 Click the **Layers** tab to select the Layers panel.

If the Layers tab is hidden, you can click **Window** and then **Layers** to open the Layers panel.

2 Click the layer to which you want to add the effect.

3 Click **Layer**.

4 Click **Layer Style**.

5 Click **Drop Shadow**.

● You can also click the **Add a Layer Style** button ([fx.]) and select **Drop Shadow**.

The Layer Style dialog box appears.

Note: *Perform Steps 6 to 11 if you want to enter your own settings. If you want to use the default settings, you can skip to Step 12.*

6 Type an Opacity value to specify the shadow's transparency.

7 Click the color swatch to select a shadow color.

Note: *The default shadow color is black.*

8 Type an Angle value to specify in which direction the shadow is displaced.

9 Type a Distance value to specify how far the shadow is displaced.

10 Type a Spread value to specify the fuzziness of the shadow's edge.

11 Type a Size value to specify the size of the shadow's edge.

12 Click **OK**.

● Photoshop creates a shadow in back of the selected layer.

● Photoshop displays the name of the style under the affected layer in the Layers panel.

Note: In this example, the effect is applied to a text layer. For more information about text, see Chapter 12.

How do I add an inner shadow to a layer?

An inner shadow creates a *cutout* effect, with the selected layer appearing to drop behind the image canvas. To apply it:

1 Click a layer in the Layers panel.

2 Click **Layer**, **Layer Style**, and then **Inner Shadow**.

● Photoshop applies the style to objects in the layer.

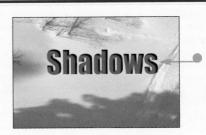

The Outer Glow effect adds
faint coloring to the outside
edge of a layer.

Apply an Outer Glow

① Click the **Layers** tab to select the
Layers panel.

If the Layers tab is hidden, you can
click **Window** and then **Layers** to
open the Layers panel.

② Click the layer to which you want
to add the style.

③ Click **Layer**.

④ Click **Layer Style**.

⑤ Click **Outer Glow**.

● You can also click fx. and select
Outer Glow.

The Layer Style dialog box
appears.

*Note: Perform Steps 6 to 10 if you want to enter
your own Outer Glow settings. If you want to use
the default settings, you can skip to Step 11.*

⑥ Type an Opacity value to specify
the glow's darkness.

⑦ Specify a Noise value to add
speckling to the glow.

⑧ Click the color swatch to choose
the color of the glow (◎ changes
to ◉).

● You can also select from a series of
preset color gradients by clicking ⊡.

⑨ Type a Spread value to determine the fuzziness of the glow.

⑩ Type a Size value to specify the size of the glow.

⑪ Click **OK**.

● Photoshop creates a glow around the outer edge of objects in the selected layer.

● Photoshop displays the name of the style under the affected layer in the Layers panel.

TIP

How do I give elements in a layer an inner glow?
The Inner Glow style adds color to the inside edge of a layer. To apply it:

① Click a layer in the Layers panel.

② Click **Layer**, **Layer Style**, and then **Inner Glow**.

● Photoshop applies the style to objects in the layer.

Apply Beveling and Embossing

You can bevel and emboss a layer to give it a three-dimensional look. This can make objects in the layer stand out and seem to rise off or sink into the screen.

Apply Beveling and Embossing

① Click the **Layers** tab to select the Layers panel.

If the Layers tab is hidden, you can click **Window** and then **Layers** to open the Layers panel.

② Click the layer to which you want to add the style.

③ Click **Layer**.

④ Click **Layer Style**.

⑤ Click **Bevel and Emboss**.

● You can also click [*fx.*] and select **Bevel and Emboss**.

The Layer Style dialog box appears.

Note: Perform Steps 6 to 9 if you want to enter your own settings. If you want to use the default settings, you can skip to Step 10.

⑥ Click here to select an effect style.

Clicking **Inner Bevel** creates a three-dimensional look.

⑦ Specify the direction of the style's shadowing (◎ changes to ◉).

⑧ Type Depth and Size values to control the magnitude of the style.

9 Specify the direction of the shading with the Angle and Altitude values.

● You can click ⊡ and select one of the Gloss Contour settings to apply abstract styles to your layer.

10 Click **OK**.

● Photoshop applies the Bevel and Emboss settings to the layer.

● Photoshop displays the name of the style under the affected layer in the Layers panel.

Note: In this example, the style is applied to a text layer. For more about text, see Chapter 12.

TIPS

When would I use the Bevel and Emboss style?
The style can be useful for creating three-dimensional buttons for Web pages or multimedia applications. For example, to create a 3-D button, you can apply Bevel and Emboss to a colored rectangle and then add type over it.

How else can I enhance the 3-D effect of Bevel and Emboss?
You can select the **Contour** option in the left-hand column of the Layer Style dialog box to darken the shading, or select **Texture** to add shadowing that is slightly wavy.

Apply Multiple Styles to a Layer

You can apply multiple styles to layers in your image. This enables you to enhance the look of your layers in complex ways.

Apply Multiple Styles to a Layer

APPLY THE FIRST STYLE

1. Click the **Layers** tab to select the Layers panel.

   If the Layers tab is hidden, you can click **Window** and then **Layers** to open the Layers panel.

2. Click the layer to which you want to add the style.

3. Click **Layer**.

4. Click **Layer Style**.

5. Click the name of the first style you want to apply.

The Layer Style dialog box appears.

6. Specify the settings for the first style.

   In this example, Gradient Overlay is applied to the layer.

APPLY THE SECOND STYLE

7 Select the name of the next style you want to apply (☐ changes to ☑).

In this example, the Bevel and Emboss style is also applied to the layer with the technique set to Smooth.

8 Specify the settings for this style.

You can apply other styles to the layer by repeating Steps **7** and **8**.

9 Click **OK**.

● Photoshop applies the styles to the layer.

● The effects appear below the selected layer in the Layers panel.

How do I turn off layer effects that I have applied?

When you apply a style to a layer, Photoshop adds the style to the Layers panel. You may have to click ▼ to see a layer's effects. You can temporarily turn off an effect by clicking the visibility icon (👁) in the Layers panel. You can turn the effect on by clicking the now-empty box again to make 👁 reappear.

Is there a quick way to remove the styles from a layer?

Select the layer and click **Layer**, **Layer Style**, and **Clear Layer Style**. Photoshop removes all the styles currently applied to the layer.

Edit a Layer Style

You can edit a layer style that you have applied to your image. This enables you to fine-tune the effect to achieve the appearance you want.

Edit a Layer Style

1 Click the **Layers** tab to select the Layers panel.

If the Layers tab is hidden, you can click **Window** and then **Layers** to open the Layers panel.

In this example, the color overlay of a layer object is edited.

2 Click the layer whose style you want to edit.

3 Click **Layer**.

4 Click **Layer Style**.

5 Click the style you want to edit.

● You can also double-click the style's name in the Layers panel.

The Layer Style dialog box opens.

● Photoshop displays the current configuration values for the style.

⑥ Edit the values in the Layer Style dialog box.

This example changes a color overlay.

● You can click another style in the Layer Style list to edit it.

⑦ Click **OK**.

● Photoshop applies the edited style to the layer.

You can edit a style as many times as you want.

sand-hands.psd @ 100% (Hand, RGB/8) * ×

TIPS

How do I keep a layer effect from accidentally being changed?

You can lock a layer and its styles by selecting the layer and clicking the **Lock** icon (🔒) in the Layers panel; the button depresses and becomes highlighted. The layer is then locked, which means that you cannot change its styles or apply additional Photoshop commands to it. You can click 🔒 again to unlock the layer.

Can I copy styles between layers?

Yes. Select the layer you want to copy from, and then click **Layer**, **Layer Styles**, and **Copy Layer Style**. To paste the style, select the destination layer, and then click **Layer**, **Layer Styles**, and **Paste Layer Style**. You can also press Alt (Option on a Mac) and then click and drag a style from one layer to another in the Layers panel to copy it.

Using the Styles Panel

You can apply a custom combination of Photoshop styles to a layer to give it a colorful or textured look. The Styles panel offers an easy way to apply such complex effects.

APPLY A STYLE FROM THE STYLES PANEL

① Click the **Layers** tab to select the Layers panel.

If the Layers tab is hidden, you can click **Window** and then **Layers** to open the Layers panel.

② Click the **Styles** tab to display Photoshop's styles.

③ Click the layer to which you want to apply the style.

If the Styles tab is hidden, you can click **Window** and then **Styles** to open the Styles panel.

④ Click a style.

● Photoshop applies the style to the selected layer.

● The style appears as a set of effects in the Layers panel.

ACCESS MORE STYLES

1 Click the Styles panel ▦.

2 Click a set of styles.

A dialog box appears and asks if you want to replace the current styles with the new set or append the new set.

3 Click **OK** or **Append**.

Photoshop places the new styles in the Styles panel.

● In this example, the new styles have been appended to the current ones.

TIP

How do I create my own custom styles?

1 Perform the techniques covered in this chapter to apply one or more effects to a layer in your image.

2 Select the layer in the Layers panel.

3 Click the Styles panel ▦ and click **New Style** from the menu.

4 In the New Style dialog box, type a name for your new style.

5 Click **OK**.

● An icon for your new style appears in the Styles panel.

Applying Filters

With Photoshop's filters, you can quickly and easily apply enhancements to your image, including artistic effects, texture effects, and distortions. Filters can help you correct defects in your images or enable you to turn a photograph into something resembling an impressionist painting. Photoshop comes with more than 100 filters; this chapter highlights only a few. For details about all the filters, see the Help documentation.

Turn an Image into a Painting

You can use many of Photoshop's artistic filters to make your image look as though it was created with a paintbrush. The Dry Brush filter, for example, applies a painted effect by converting similarly colored areas in your image to solid colors.

The Dry Brush filter uses the Filter Gallery interface. For more information about the Filter Gallery, see the section "Apply Multiple Filters."

Turn an Image into a Painting

① Select the layer to which you want to apply the filter.

In this example, the image has a single Background layer.

To apply the filter to just part of your image, make a selection with a selection tool.

Note: *For more about layers, see Chapter 8. See Chapter 4 for more on using the selection tools.*

② Click **Filter**.

③ Click **Artistic**.

④ Click **Dry Brush**.

The Filter Gallery dialog box appears with the Dry Brush filter selected.

The left pane displays a preview of the filter's effect.

The middle pane enables you to select a different artistic or other type of filter.

● You can also select a different filter by clicking ▾ in the right pane.

⑤ Fine-tune the filter effect by typing values for Brush Size, Brush Detail, and Texture.

● You can close the middle pane by
clicking ⊼.

On a Mac, you can close the
middle pane by clicking ▲
(▲ changes to ▼).

This example shows how to
thicken the Dry Brush effect by
increasing Brush Size and
decreasing Brush Detail.

⑥ Click **OK**.

Photoshop applies the filter.

TIPS

What does the Sponge filter do?
The Sponge filter reduces detail and
modifies the shapes in an image to
create the effect you get when
applying a damp sponge to a wet
painting. Apply it by clicking **Filter**,
Artistic, and then **Sponge**. Note that
this effect is different from that of the
Sponge tool (🔲). See Chapter 7 for more about the
Sponge tool.

**How can I make the objects
in my image look like they
are molded from plastic?**
The Plastic Wrap filter gives
objects a shiny appearance, as
if wrapped in heat-shrink
plastic. To apply this effect, click
Filter, **Artistic**, and then **Plastic
Wrap**. You can adjust how well the plastic wrap
reflects light, its shininess, and its smoothness.

Blur an Image

Photoshop's blur filters reduce the amount of detail in your image. The Gaussian Blur filter has an advantage over other blur filters in that you can control the amount of blur added.

① Select the layer to which you want to apply the filter.

To apply the filter to just part of your image, make a selection with a selection tool.

Note: *For more about layers, see Chapter 8. To learn about the selection tools, see Chapter 4.*

● In this example, the scenery around the center grapes has been selected.

② Click **Filter**.

③ Click **Blur**.

④ Click **Gaussian Blur**.

The Gaussian Blur dialog box appears.

● A preview of the filter's effect appears here.

● You can click ➕ or ➖ to zoom in or out.

⑤ Select **Preview** to see the effect in the image window (☐ changes to ☑).

⑥ Click and drag the **Radius** slider (△) to control the amount of blur added.

In this example, boosting the Radius value increases the amount of blur.

⑦ Click **OK**.

Photoshop applies the filter.

TIP

How do I add directional blurring to an image?

You can add directional blur to your image with the Motion Blur filter. This can add a sense of motion to your image. To apply the filter:

① Click **Filter**, **Blur**, and then **Motion Blur**.

② In the Motion Blur dialog box, adjust the angle and distance to customize the blur's direction and intensity.

③ Click **OK** to apply the filter.

Sharpen an Image

Photoshop's sharpen filters intensify the detail and reduce blurring in your image. The Unsharp Mask filter has advantages over other sharpen filters in that you can control the amount of sharpening you apply.

Sharpen an Image

1 Select the layer to which you want to apply the filter.

In this example, the filter is applied to the layer that contains the donkey.

To apply the filter to just part of your image, you can make a selection with a selection tool.

Note: *For more about layers, see Chapter 8. For more on using the selection tools, see Chapter 4.*

2 Click **Filter**.

3 Click **Sharpen**.

4 Click **Unsharp Mask**.

The Unsharp Mask dialog box appears.

● A preview of the filter's effect appears here.

● You can click + or − to zoom in or out.

5 Select **Preview** to see the effect in the main window (changes to).

6 Click and drag the sliders ( ) to control the amount of sharpening you apply to the image.

Amount controls the overall amount of sharpening.

Radius controls whether sharpening is confined to edges in the image (low Radius setting) or added across the entire image (high Radius setting).

Threshold controls the amount of contrast that must be present for an edge to be recognized and sharpened.

⑦ Click **OK**.

Photoshop applies the filter.

When should I apply sharpening?

It is a good idea to sharpen an image after you enlarge it because enlarging can cause blurring. Applying the Unsharp Mask filter can also help clarify scanned images.

How can I remove a specific type of blurring from my image?

The Smart Sharpen filter gives you additional control over the sharpening applied to your image. You can specify that it remove blurring applied by the Gaussian Blur, Lens Blur, or Motion Blur filter. To access it, click **Filter**, **Sharpen**, and **Smart Sharpen**. You can also add blurring in the first place as a Smart Filter, which gives you the option of removing the filter later. For details, see "Using Smart Filters."

Distort an Image

Photoshop's distort filters stretch and squeeze areas of your image. For example, the Spherize filter produces a fun-house effect, making your image look like it is being reflected in a mirrored sphere.

You can also distort an image by using the Distort command, located under the Image menu. See Chapter 5 for more information.

Distort an Image

① Select the layer to which you want to apply the filter.

To apply the filter to just part of your image, make a selection with a selection tool.

Note: *For more about layers, see Chapter 8. For more on using the selection tools, see Chapter 4.*

● In this example, one of the glass jars is selected.

② Click **Filter**.

③ Click **Distort**.

④ Click **Spherize**.

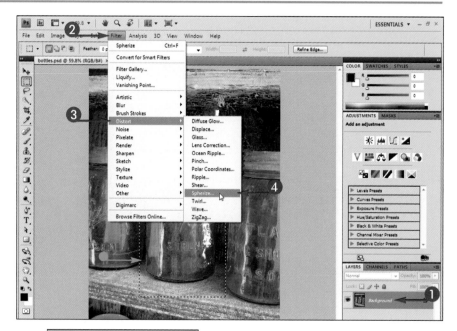

The Spherize dialog box appears.

● A preview of the filter's effect appears here.

● You can click ⊞ or ⊟ to zoom in or out.

⑤ Click and drag the **Amount** slider (△) to control the amount of distortion added.

In this example, the intensity of the spherize effect has been decreased.

6 Click **OK**.

Photoshop applies the filter.

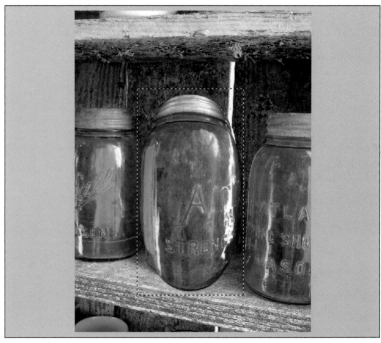

TIPS

What happens when I type a negative value in the Amount field of the Spherize dialog box?

A negative value "squeezes" the shapes in your image instead of expanding them. The Pinch filter — which you can also find under the Filter and Distort menu selections — produces a similar effect.

How can I quickly add wild special effects to my images?

Many of the filters in the Stylize menu produce out-of-this-world effects. The Emboss and Solarize filters are two examples. Click **Filter** and then **Stylize** to access them.

Add Noise to an Image

Filters in the Noise menu add or remove graininess. You can add graininess to your image with the Add Noise filter.

Add Noise to an Image

① Select the layer to which you want to apply the filter.

This image has a single Background layer.

To apply the filter to just part of your image, make a selection with a selection tool.

Note: For more about layers, see Chapter 8. For more on using the selection tools, see Chapter 4.

② Click **Filter**.

③ Click **Noise**.

④ Click **Add Noise**.

The Add Noise dialog box appears.

● A preview appears here.

● You can click ⊞ or ⊟ to zoom in or out.

⑤ Select **Preview** to see the effect in the main window (☐ changes to ☑).

⑥ Click and drag the **Amount** slider (△) to control the amount of noise added.

⑦ Select the way you want the noise distributed (◯ changes to ◉).

The Uniform option spreads the noise more evenly than the Gaussian option.

In this example, the Amount value has been increased.

⑧ Click **OK**.

Photoshop applies the filter.

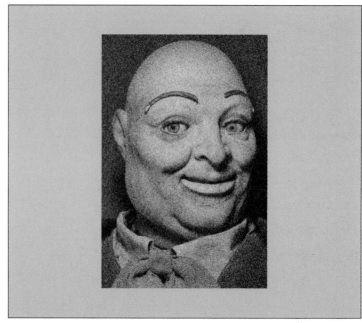

TIP

What does the Monochromatic setting in the Add Noise dialog box do?

If you select **Monochromatic** (☐ changes to ☑), Photoshop adds noise by lightening or darkening pixels in your image. Pixel hues stay the same. At high settings with the Monochromatic setting on, the filter produces a television-static effect.

Turn an Image into Shapes

The pixelate filters divide areas of your image into solid-colored dots or shapes. The Crystallize filter, one example of a pixelate filter, re-creates your image using colored polygons.

① Select the layer to which you want to apply the filter.

In this example, the image has a single Background layer.

To apply the filter to just part of your image, make a selection with a selection tool.

Note: *For more about layers, see Chapter 8. For more on using the selection tools, see Chapter 4.*

② Click **Filter**.

③ Click **Pixelate**.

④ Click **Crystallize**.

The Crystallize dialog box appears.

● A preview of the filter's effect appears here.

● You can click ⊞ or ⊟ to zoom in or out.

⑤ Click and drag the **Cell Size** slider (△) to adjust the size of the shapes.

The size can range from 3 to 300.

In this example, the Cell Size value has been increased.

6 Click **OK**.

Photoshop applies the filter.

What does the Mosaic filter do?

The Mosaic filter converts your image to a set of solid-color squares. You can control the size of the squares in the filter's dialog box. Apply the filter by clicking **Filter**, **Pixelate**, and then **Mosaic**.

What does the Stained Glass filter do?

The Stained Glass filter converts small areas of your image to different solid-color shapes, similar to those you may see in a stained-glass window. A foreground-color border separates the shapes. You can adjust the thickness of the border, along with cell size and light intensity. Apply this filter by clicking **Filter**, **Texture**, and then **Stained Glass**.

Turn an Image into a Charcoal Sketch

The sketch filters add outlining effects to your image. The Charcoal filter, for example, makes an image look as if you sketched it by using charcoal on paper.

The Charcoal filter uses the Filter Gallery interface. For more information about the Filter Gallery, see the section "Apply Multiple Filters."

Turn an Image into a Charcoal Sketch

① Select the layer to which you want to apply the filter.

In this example, the image has a single Background layer.

To apply the filter to just part of your image, make a selection with a selection tool.

Note: For more about layers, see Chapter 8. For more on using the selection tools, see Chapter 4.

② Click **Filter**.

③ Click **Sketch**.

④ Click **Charcoal**.

The Filter Gallery dialog box appears with the Charcoal filter selected.

The left pane displays a preview of the filter's effect.

The middle pane enables you to select a different Sketch or other type of filter.

● You can also select a different filter by clicking ⏷ in the right pane.

⑤ Click and drag the sliders (△) to control the filter's effect.

● You can close the middle pane by clicking ⏶.

On a Mac, you can close the middle pane by clicking ⏶ (⏶ changes to ⏷).

⑥ Click **OK**.

Photoshop applies the filter.

In this example, the thickness of the charcoal strokes has been increased, and the Light/Dark Balance setting has also been increased.

● Photoshop uses the current foreground color as the charcoal and the current background color as the canvas.

Note: For more about choosing the foreground and background colors, see Chapter 6.

What does the Photocopy filter do?

The Photocopy filter converts shadows and midtones in your image to the foreground color in the toolbox and highlights in your image to the background color. The result is an image that looks photocopied. To apply the Photocopy filter:

❶ Follow Steps **1** to **4** in this section, but in Step **4**, click **Photocopy**.

The Filter Gallery appears with the Photocopy filter selected.

❷ Adjust the detail and the darkness of the filter effect.

❸ Click **OK**.

Photoshop applies the filter.

Apply Glowing Edges to an Image

The Glowing Edges filter, one example of a stylize filter, applies a neon effect to the edges in your image. Areas between the edges turn black. Other stylize filters produce similarly extreme artistic effects.

The Glowing Edges filter uses the Filter Gallery interface. For more information about the Filter Gallery, see the section "Apply Multiple Filters."

Apply Glowing Edges to an Image

① Select the layer to which you want to apply the filter.

In this example, the image has a single Background layer.

To apply the filter to just part of your image, make a selection with a selection tool.

Note: For more about layers, see Chapter 8. For more on using the selection tools, see Chapter 4.

② Click **Filter**.

③ Click **Stylize**.

④ Click **Glowing Edges**.

The Filter Gallery dialog box appears with the Glowing Edges filter selected.

The left pane displays a preview of the filter's effect.

The middle pane enables you to select a different filter.

● You can also select a different filter by clicking ▼ in the right pane.

⑤ Click and drag the sliders (△) to control the intensity of the glow you add to the edges in the image.

● You can close the middle pane by clicking 🔼.

On a Mac, you can close the middle pane by clicking 🔺 (🔺 changes to 🔻).

In this example, the Edge Width and Edge Brightness values are increased to intensify the neon effect.

6 Click **OK**.

Photoshop applies the filter.

What is the Find Edges filter?

The Find Edges filter is similar to the Glowing Edges filter except that it places white pixels between the edges in your image. Find Edges is a one-step filter, which means that you cannot fine-tune its effects in a dialog box before you apply it. To apply the filter:

1 Click **Filter**.

2 Click **Stylize**.

3 Click **Find Edges**.

Photoshop applies the filter.

Add Texture to an Image

You can overlay different textures on your image with the Texturizer filter. The other texture filters enable you to apply other patterns.

The Texturizer filter uses the Filter Gallery interface. For more information about the Filter Gallery, see the section "Apply Multiple Filters."

① Select the layer to which you want to apply the filter.

To apply the filter to just part of your image, make a selection with a selection tool.

In this example, the image has a single Background layer.

Note: For more about layers, see Chapter 8. For more on using the selection tools, see Chapter 4.

② Click **Filter**.

③ Click **Texture**.

④ Click **Texturizer**.

The Filter Gallery dialog box appears with the Texturizer filter selected.

The left pane displays a preview of the filter's effect.

The middle pane enables you to select a different texture or other type of filter.

● You can also select a different filter by clicking ⏷ in the right pane.

⑤ Click here and select a texture to apply.

6 Click and drag the sliders (◁) to control the size and intensity of the overlaid texture.

7 Click here and select a **Light** direction.

● You can close the middle pane by clicking ⊼.

On a Mac, you can close the middle pane by clicking ▲ (▲ changes to ▼).

8 Click **OK**.

Photoshop applies the filter.

TIP

What is a lens flare, and how can I add it to an image?

Lens flare is the extra flash of light that sometimes appears in a photo when too much light enters a camera lens. Photographers try to avoid this effect, but you can add it to make your digital image look more like an old-fashioned photograph. To apply the filter, follow these steps:

1 Click **Filter**, **Render**, and then **Lens Flare**.

2 In the Lens Flare dialog box, click and drag △ to control the brightness.

3 Click and drag + to position the lens flare in your image.

4 Click **OK** to apply the filter.

Offset
an Image

The filters in the Other submenu produce interesting effects that do not fall under the other menu descriptions. For example, you can shift your image horizontally or vertically in the image window using the Other submenu's Offset filter.

Offset an Image

1 Select the layer to which you want to apply the filter.

In this example, the image has a single Background layer.

To apply the filter to just part of your image, make a selection with a selection tool.

Note: For more about layers, see Chapter 8. For more on using the selection tools, see Chapter 4.

2 Click **Filter**.

3 Click **Other**.

4 Click **Offset**.

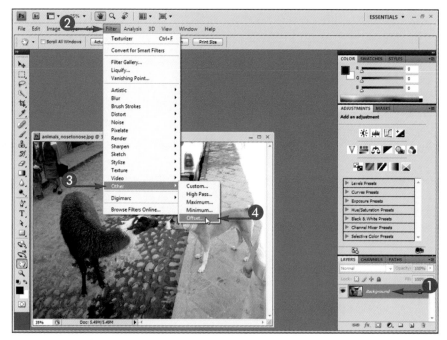

The Offset dialog box appears.

5 Type a horizontal offset.

6 Type a vertical offset.

7 Select how you want Photoshop to treat pixels at the edge (◉ changes to ◉).

8 Click **OK**.

Because a positive value was entered in the horizontal field, the image has been shifted horizontally to the right.

Wrap Around was selected in Step **7**, so the pixels cropped from the right edge of the image reappear on the left edge.

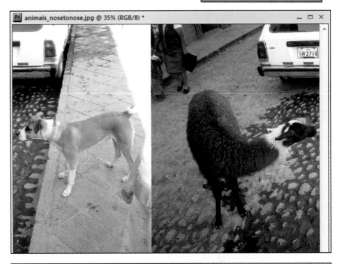

In this example, the same offset is applied but with Repeat Edge Pixels selected in Step **7**, which creates a streaked effect at the left edge.

 TIP

How do I make a seamless tile?

Seamless tiles are images that when laid side by side leave no noticeable seam where they meet. They are often used as background images for Web pages. To create a seamless tile, follow these steps:

1 Open an image that has even textures and coloring.

2 Perform Steps **1** to **8** in this section.

3 Clean up the resulting seams with the **Clone Stamp** tool (🔲).

The resulting image tiles seamlessly.

Using the Liquify Filter

Photoshop's Liquify tools enable you to dramatically warp areas of your image. The tools are useful for making your image look like it is melting.

Using the Liquify Filter

① Select the layer to which you want to apply the Liquify filter.

In this example, the image has a single Background layer.

To apply the filter to just part of your image, make a selection with a selection tool.

Note: *For more about layers, see Chapter 8. For more on using the selection tools, see Chapter 4.*

② Click **Filter**.

③ Click **Liquify**.

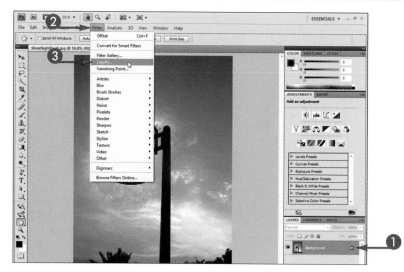

The Liquify dialog box appears.

④ Type a Brush Size from 1 to 600.

⑤ Type a Brush Pressure, or strength, from 1 to 100.

⑥ Click a liquify tool.

This example uses the Forward Warp tool ().

⑦ Click and drag inside the image preview box.

Photoshop liquifies the image where you drag the brush.

● You can click **Reconstruct** to change the image back to its original state, step by step.

● You can select the **Show Mesh** option (☐ changes to ☑) to overlay a grid so you can measure your changes.

⑧ Click **OK**.

Photoshop applies the Liquify effect to your image.

 TIP

What do some of the different Liquify tools do?

	Tool	Description
	Forward Warp tool	Pushes pixels in the direction you drag.
	Reconstruct tool	Restores pixels to their original state.
	Twirl Clockwise tool	Twirls pixels clockwise. Press Alt (Option) to twirl pixels counterclockwise.
	Pucker tool	Pushes pixels toward the brush center.
	Bloat tool	Pushes pixels away from the brush center.
	Push Left tool	Pushes pixels to the left of the cursor as you drag.
	Mirror tool	Reflects pixels as you drag.
	Turbulence tool	Mimics a roiling liquid.

Apply Multiple Filters

You can apply more than one filter to an image using the Filter Gallery interface. The interface enables you to view a variety of filter effects and apply them in combination.

Many filters open the Filter Gallery interface when you apply them, including Dry Brush, Charcoal Sketch, Glowing Edges, and Texturizer. See previous sections in this chapter for more information about these filters.

Note that not all of the effects listed under Photoshop's Filter menu appear in the Filter Gallery.

Apply Multiple Filters

1 Select the layer to which you want to apply the filters.

In this example, the image has a single Background layer.

To apply the filters to just part of your image, make a selection with a selection tool.

Note: For more about layers, see Chapter 8. For more on using the selection tools, see Chapter 4.

2 Click **Filter**.

3 Click **Filter Gallery**.

The Filter Gallery dialog box appears with the most recently applied filter selected.

The left pane displays a preview of the filtered image.

4 Click 📁 to display filters from a category (📁 changes to 📂).

5 Click a thumbnail to apply a filter.

● The filter appears in the filter list.

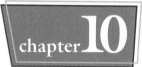

6 Click the **New Effect Layer** button ().

7 Click ☐ to display filters from another category (☐ changes to ☐).

8 Click a thumbnail to apply another filter.

● The new effect appears in the list.

You can repeat Steps **6** to **8** to apply additional filters.

9 Click **OK**.

Photoshop applies the filters.

How can I turn off filters in the Filter Gallery?
Currently applied filters appear in a list in the lower right corner of the Filter Gallery. You can click 👁 to temporarily hide a filter in the list. A hidden filter's effects are not applied to the preview in the left pane of the Filter Gallery, nor are they applied to the image when you click **OK**. You can click 🗑 to delete a filter entirely from the list.

Using Smart Filters

Filters that you apply to Smart Objects in your images are known as Smart Filters. You can edit Smart Filters and turn them on and off as you continue to make changes to your image. You cannot do this with filters applied to normal layers.

For more information about Smart Objects, see Chapter 8.

Using Smart Filters

APPLY A SMART FILTER

1 Select the Smart Object to which you want to apply a filter.

2 Click **Filter**.

3 Click a filter category.

4 Click a filter.

The dialog box for that filter appears.

5 Adjust the filter settings.

6 Click **OK**.

● Photoshop applies the filter to the Smart Object in the image.

● The filter appears in the Layers panel.

You can repeat Steps **2** to **6** to apply multiple Smart Filters to the Smart Object.

TURN OFF A SMART FILTER

1 Click 👁 next to the Smart Filter.
👁 changes to ☐ and Photoshop turns off the Smart Filter.

You can click ☐ to turn the Smart Filter back on.

● You can click 👁 next to Smart Filters to turn off all the Smart Filters for a layer.

EDIT A SMART FILTER

1 Double-click a Smart Filter.

Photoshop opens the dialog box for the Smart Filter.

2 Edit the filter settings.

3 Click **OK**.

Photoshop applies the edited settings.

TIP

How can I control how a Smart Filter is blended with the Smart Objects in my image?

1 Double-click **Filter Blending Options** (🔲) next to a Smart Filter.

2 Click to select a blending mode.

● You can control the strength of the applied effect.

3 Click **OK**.

Photoshop applies the Smart Filter with the updated blending.

Drawing Shapes

Photoshop offers a variety of tools for drawing geometric and abstract shapes. Other tools let you edit the lines that bound your shapes, or change the colors with which the shapes are filled. You can also use the tools to draw lines that have arrowheads at their ends.

Draw a Shape

You can add solid shapes to your image using Photoshop's many shape tools. These tools make it easy to create geometric decorations for your photos or buttons for your Web site.

Photoshop's shapes are *vector-based*, which means you can resize them without loss of quality.

Draw a Shape

DRAW A SOLID SHAPE

1 Click the **Shape** tool (□).

Note: The tool icon may differ, depending on the type of shape you drew last.

2 Click a shape in the options bar.

3 Click the **Shape Layers** icon (□) in the options bar.

4 Click the **Color** box to select a fill color for the shape.

Note: For details on selecting colors, see Chapter 6.

5 Click and drag to draw the shape.

Photoshop draws the shape and fills it with the specified color.

● The shape appears in a new layer in the Layers panel.

Note: For more about layers, see Chapter 8.

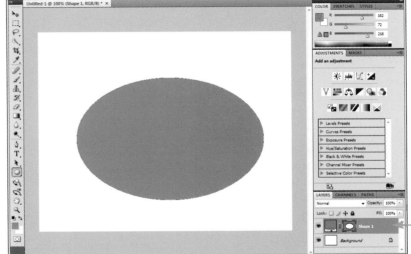

DRAW A STYLIZED SHAPE

① Click a shape button.

② Click here and then select a style for your shape.

Photoshop offers a variety of colorful 3-D styles.

③ Click and drag to draw the shape.

Photoshop draws the shape and applies the specified style.

● The shape appears in a new layer in the Layers panel.

Note: For more about layers, see Chapter 8; for more about styles, see Chapter 9.

● You can move the shape by selecting its layer and using the **Move** tool ().

Note: For more about the Move tool, see Chapter 5.

TIPS

How do I resize a shape after I draw it?

Click the shape's layer and then click the **Shape** tool (□). Click **Edit**, **Transform Path**, and then a transform command. You can resize the shape just as you would a selection. See Chapter 5 for details on transforming selections.

How do I overlap shapes in interesting ways?

To determine how overlapping shapes interact, click one of the following options in the options bar before drawing:

	Add to Shape Area	Combines a shape area with another shape area
	Subtract from Shape Area	Cuts a shape area out of another shape area
	Intersect Shape Areas	Keeps the area where shapes intersect
	Exclude Overlapping Shape Areas	Keeps the area where shapes do not overlap

Draw a Custom Shape

You can use the Custom Shape tool to draw a variety of interesting predefined shapes, including animals, frames, and talk bubbles.

Draw a Custom Shape

1 Click ⬜.

2 Click the **Custom Shape** button (🖼️) in the options bar.

3 Click the **Shape** ▾.

4 Click the **Option** arrow (▶).

5 Click a shape category.

A dialog box appears and asks if you want to replace the current shapes.

● You can click **Append** to append the new shapes to the current shapes.

6 Click **OK**.

Photoshop replaces the old shapes with your current shapes.

7 Click a shape.

8 Click the **Color** box to select a color for the shape.

Note: For details on selecting colors, see Chapter 6.

9 Click and drag to draw the shape.

Photoshop draws the shape and fills it with the specified color.

● The shape appears in a new layer in the Layers panel.

Note: For more about layers, see Chapter 8.

● You can move the shape by selecting its layer and using .

Note: For more about the Move tool, see Chapter 5.

TIPS

How do I apply a shadow behind a shape?

You can apply a Drop Shadow style to the shape. Select your shape layer in the Layers panel, and then click **Layer**, **Layer Style**, and **Drop Shadow**. A dialog box appears that enables you to customize the shadowing. For more about applying styles, see Chapter 9.

How do I overlay text on a shape?

You can click the **Type** tool (T), click your shape, and then type the text you want to overlay. This can be useful when you want to label buttons you create with the Shape tool. You will probably want to select a color for your text that contrasts with the color of your shape. For more about applying type, see Chapter 12.

247

Draw a Straight Line

You can draw a straight line using Photoshop's Shape tool. You can point out elements in your image by customizing the line with arrowheads.

① Click ▣.

Note: *The tool icon may differ, depending on the type of shape you drew last.*

② Make sure the **Shape Layers** icon (▣) is selected in the options bar.

③ Click the **Line** button (◥).

④ Click here and then select the **Start** and/or **End** option (☐ changes to ☑) to add arrowheads to your line.

● You can also specify the size and shape of the arrowheads by typing values here.

⑤ Press Enter (Return on a Mac) to close the menu.

⑥ Type a line weight.

⑦ Click here and then click a style for your line.

● The default style (▨) creates a plain, solid line.

⑧ Press **Enter** (**Return** on a Mac) to close the menu.

● You can click the **Color** box to select a different line color.

⑨ Click and drag to draw the line.

● Photoshop places the line in its own layer.

Note: For more about layers, see Chapter 8.

● You can move the shape by selecting its layer and using ⊹.

Note: For more about the Move tool, see Chapter 5.

TIPS

How do I draw a horizontal or vertical line?

Press **Shift** as you click and drag to create your line. You can also use this technique to drag lines at 45-degree angles.

How do I resize a line?

You can select the layer containing the line, click **Image**, and then click **Free Transform**. A bounding box appears around the line. You can click and drag the handles on the sides and corners to resize the line.

Draw a Shape with the Pen

With the Pen tool, you can create shapes by drawing the lines yourself. This enables you to make shapes that are not included in Photoshop's predefined menus.

Draw a Shape with the Pen

USING THE REGULAR PEN

1. Click the **Pen** tool (![pen icon]).

2. Click the **Shape Layers** icon (![icon]) in the options bar.

3. Click the **Color** box to select a color for the shape.

Note: For details on selecting colors, see Chapter 6.

4. Click inside your image to set an initial anchor point.

5. Continue clicking to set additional anchor points and define the shape.

6. Click the initial anchor point to close the shape.

    Photoshop draws a straight-sided shape.

● Photoshop places the shape in its own layer.

    You can create curved paths if you click and drag with ![pen icon].

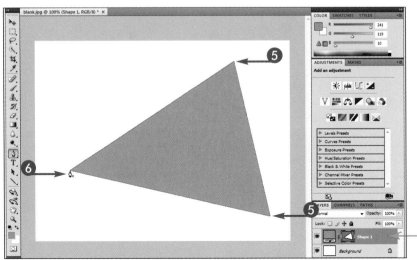

USING THE FREEFORM PEN

1 Click and hold .

2 Click the **Freeform Pen** tool ( ) from the list that appears.

● You can also select the tool from the options bar.

3 Click and drag inside your image.

Photoshop draws a free-form line.

4 Drag to the starting point of the line.

Photoshop completes the shape.

Alternatively, you can release the mouse, and Photoshop completes your shape with a straight line.

● Photoshop places the shape in its own layer.

TIP

How can I trace an object in my image using the Pen tool?
If the object has well-defined edges, you can trace it using the Freeform Pen tool ( ) with the Magnetic option selected in the options bar (changes to). The tool works similarly to the Magnetic Lasso tool ( ). For more on using the Magnetic Lasso, see Chapter 4.

Edit a Shape

You can edit shapes by manipulating their anchor points. This lets you fine-tune the geometries of your shapes.

You can edit shapes drawn with Photoshop's predefined shape tools or the Pen tool.

For more shape-editing techniques, see Photoshop's Help documentation.

Edit a Shape

MOVE AN ANCHOR POINT

1. Click and hold the **Path Selection** tool ().

2. Click the **Direct Selection** tool () from the list that appears.

3. Click the edge of a shape to select it.

   Photoshop shows the anchor points that make up the shape.

4. Click and drag an anchor point.

Photoshop moves the anchor point, changing the geometry of the shape.

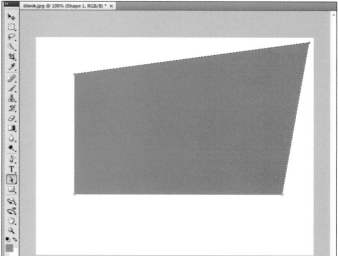

BEND A STRAIGHT SEGMENT

1 Click and hold .

2 Click the **Add Anchor Point** tool (◊⁺) from the list that appears.

3 Click a straight line between two anchor points.

Photoshop adds an anchor point to the line.

4 Click the anchor point and drag.

5 Release the mouse.

Photoshop turns the straight line into a curved line.

You can use this technique to create a concave or convex curve.

TIPS

How do I edit curved lines?

If you click an anchor point on a curved line using the Direct Selection tool (▷), direction lines appear to the sides of the anchor point. You can click and drag the ends of the direction lines to edit the curve on each side of the anchor point. You can also click and drag the curves themselves with ▷.

How do I turn a shape layer into a regular layer?

You can turn a shape layer into a regular layer by *rasterizing* it. Click the shape layer, and then click **Layer**, **Rasterize**, and **Shape**. After rasterizing, the shape's anchor points are no longer accessible. This means you cannot change the geometry of the shape by editing the anchor points. Most of Photoshop's filter commands require you to rasterize a shape before you can apply the commands to it. For more about filters, see Chapter 10.

Adding and Manipulating Type

You can add letters and words to your photos and illustrations. Photoshop lets you add type to your images and precisely control the type's appearance and layout. You can also modify your type using Photoshop's styles.

Add Type to an Image

Adding type enables you to label elements in your image or use letters and words in artistic ways. You can customize your type in Photoshop using the different fonts installed on your computer.

1 Click the **Type** tool (T).

2 Click where you want the new type to appear.

Note: *You can also create a bounding box by drawing a shape. See Chapter 11 for details.*

3 Click ⊡ and select a font, style, and size for your type.

Note: *To apply a shape using type, you can choose a shape-oriented font such as Wingdings.*

4 Click the color swatch to select a color for your type.

Photoshop applies the foreground color by default.

Note: *See Chapter 6 for more about selecting colors.*

5 Type your text.

To create a line break, press Enter (Return on a Mac).

6 When you finish typing your text, click ✓ or press Enter (⌘+Return on a Mac).

● Photoshop places the type in its own layer.

● You can click the alignment buttons to left-align (▤), center (▤), or right-align (▤) your type.

How do I create vertical type?

If you click and hold the **Type** tool (T), a list that contains the Vertical Type tool (T) appears. You can then use the tool to create up-and-down type. When using the regular Type tool, you can click the **Change Orientation** button (T) in the options bar to change horizontal type to vertical, and vice versa. Note that with vertical type, lines go from right to left.

How do I reposition my type?

You can use the Move tool (▸+) to move the layer that contains the type. Click the layer of type, click ▸+, and then click and drag to reposition your type. For more about moving a layer, see Chapter 8.

Add Type in a Bounding Box

You can add type inside a *bounding box*, which is a rectangular container for text, to constrain where the type appears and how it wraps.

① Click T.

② Click and drag inside the image to define the bounding box.

③ Click and drag the handles (□) of the bounding box to adjust its dimensions.

④ Click and drag the center point (⊹) of the bounding box to move the box.

⑤ Click ▾ and select the formatting of the type to be added.

6 Type your text.

Your text appears inside the bounding box.

When a line of text hits the edge of the bounding box, it automatically wraps to the next line.

Photoshop also automatically adds hyphenation.

Note: *You can turn off hyphenation in the Paragraph panel. See the tip below for details.*

7 When you finish typing your text, click ✓ or press Enter (⌘+Return on a Mac).

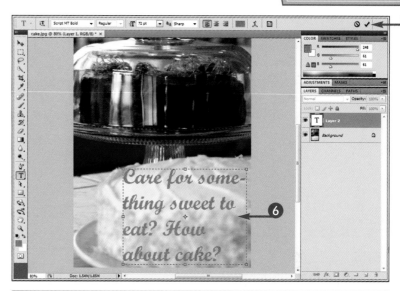

The bounding box disappears.

● To make the box reappear in order to change its dimensions, click T and click the text.

How do I format paragraph text inside a bounding box?
Follow these steps:

1 Click T.

2 Click the text inside the box.

3 Click **Window** and then **Paragraph**.

The Paragraph panel appears.

4 Type values or click the various tools to control the alignment, indenting, and hyphenation of the text inside the bounding box.

Change the Formatting of Type

You can change the font, style, size, and other characteristics of your type.

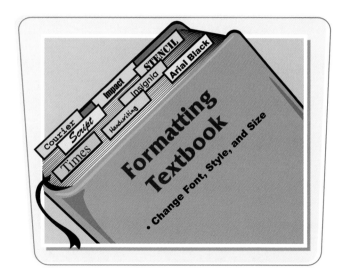

Change the Formatting of Type

1. Click **T**.

2. Click the type layer that you want to edit.

   If the Layers panel is not visible, you can click **Window** and then **Layers** to view it.

3. Click and drag to select some type.

4. Click **Window** and then **Character**.

   The Character panel appears.

● You can also make many formatting changes in the options bar.

5. Click ▾.

   Photoshop displays the names and previews of available fonts.

   You can change the size of the font previews in the Type preferences dialog box by clicking **Edit** (**Photoshop** on a Mac), **Preferences**, and then **Type**.

6. Click a font.

⑦ Click ▾ and select the type's style.

⑧ Click ▾ and select the type's size.

⑨ Type percentage values here to stretch or shrink your type.

You can click other options in the panel to add more formatting.

⑩ Click here to close the panel.

⑪ When you finish formatting your text, click ✓ or press Enter (⌘+Return on a Mac).

● Photoshop applies the formatting to your type.

TIPS

How do I edit the content of my type?

With the type's layer selected in the Layers panel, you can click the **Type** tool (T) and click inside the text. Press Delete to delete letters, or you can type new ones. You can press ←, →, ↑, or ↓ to move the cursor inside your type.

How can I check the spelling of my text?

Select your type layer in the Layers panel, click **Edit**, and then click **Check Spelling**. Photoshop compares your text with the text in its dictionary. It flags words it does not recognize and suggests replacements.

Change the Color of Type

You can change the color of your type to make it blend or contrast with the rest of the image.

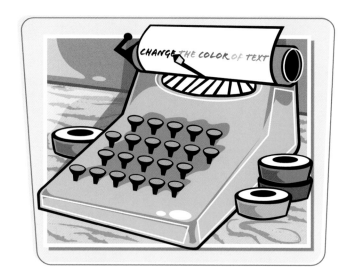

Change the Color of Type

① Click T.

② Click the type layer that you want to edit.

If the Layers panel is not visible, you can click **Window** and then **Layers** to view it.

③ Click and drag to select some text.

● You can double-click the layer thumbnail to select all the type.

④ Click the color swatch in the options bar.

The Select Text Color dialog box appears.

⑤ Click a color.

● You can click and drag the slider () to change the colors that Photoshop displays in the selection box.

⑥ Click **OK**.

⑦ Click ✔ or press Enter (⌘ + Return on a Mac).

● Photoshop changes the text to the new color.

TIPS

What is anti-aliasing?
Anti-aliasing is the process of adding semitransparent pixels to curved edges in digital images to make the edges appear smoother. You can apply anti-aliasing to type to improve its appearance. Text that you do not anti-alias can sometimes look jagged. You can control the presence and style of your type's anti-aliasing with the [aa] menu in the options bar.

How can I apply a color gradient to my type?
You can apply the Gradient Overlay style to your type. Click the type layer and then click **Layer**, **Layer Style**, and **Gradient Overlay**. A dialog box appears, allowing you to define the gradient settings. For more about styles, see Chapter 9.

Apply a Style to Type

You can easily apply a style to type to give it a colorful or 3-D appearance. After you apply a style, you can still edit the type using the type tools.

For more about styles, see Chapter 9.

Apply a Style to Type

1. Select the type layer to which you want to apply a style.

   If the Layers panel is not visible, you can click **Window** and then **Layers** to view it.

2. Click **Layer**.

3. Click **Layer Style**.

4. Click a style.

● You can also click the **Add a Layer Style** icon (*fx*) in the Layers panel to select a style.

The Layer Style dialog box appears.

5 Adjust the settings to produce the effect you want.

● You can apply multiple styles by selecting the options on the left (☐ changes to ☑).

Note: See Chapter 9 for details about applying multiple styles.

6 Click **OK**.

● Photoshop applies the style to the type.

● Photoshop displays the name of the style under the type layer in the Layers panel.

TIPS

How do I convert my type to a shape?

Click the type layer in the Layers panel. Then click **Layer**, **Type**, and **Convert to Shape**. After you convert your type to a shape, you can edit the outline of the type using the Direct Selection tool (�) and other shape tools but you can no longer edit the text with the Type tool. For more about editing shapes, see Chapter 11.

How can I create semitransparent type?

Select the type layer in the Layers panel and then reduce the layer's opacity to less than 100 percent. This makes the type semitransparent. For details about changing opacity, see Chapter 8.

Warp Type

You can easily bend and distort layers of type with Photoshop's Warp feature. This can make words look wrinkled or like they are blowing in the wind.

You can also warp type using Photoshop's transformation tools. See Chapter 6 for details.

You can also warp type using Photoshop's transformation tools. See Chapter 6 for details.

Warp Type

① Click T.

② Click the type layer that you want to warp.

  If the Layers panel is not visible, you can click **Window** and then **Layers** to view it.

③ Click the **Create Warped Text** button (𝕴).

  The Warp Text dialog box appears.

④ Click the **Style** ⬛ (⬛ on a Mac).

⑤ Click a warp style.

⑥ Select an orientation for the warp effect (◯ changes to ◉).

⑦ Adjust the Bend and Distortion values by clicking and dragging the sliders (△).

  The Bend and Distortion values determine the strength of the warp. At 0 percent for all values, no warp is applied.

⑧ Click **OK**.

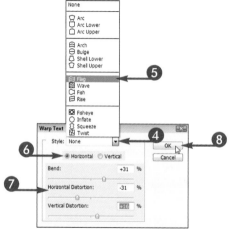

● Photoshop warps the text.

You can edit the format, color, and other characteristics of the type after you apply the warp.

TIP

How do I unwarp text?

Follow these steps:

1 Click T.

2 Click the type layer that you want to unwarp.

3 Click the **Create Warp Text** button (⬛).

4 In the Warp Text dialog box, click the **Style** ⬛ (⬛ on a Mac) and select **None**.

5 Click **OK**.

Photoshop unwarps your type.

CHAPTER
13

Automating Your Work

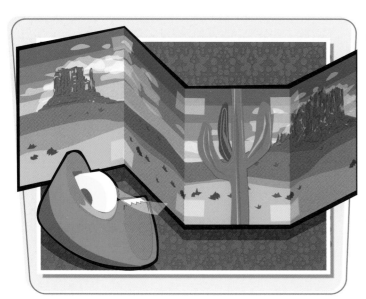

With Photoshop's Action commands, you can automate repetitive imaging tasks by saving sequences of commands and applying them automatically to many image files. Other Photoshop commands enable you to streamline your work by helping you create Web photo galleries, picture packages, contact sheets, and panoramas.

Record an Action

You can record a sequence of commands as an action and replay it on other image files. This can save you time when you have a task in Photoshop that you need to repeat.

After you record an action, you can play it. See the section "Play an Action" for more information.

Record an Action

① Click **Window**.

② Click **Actions**.

The Actions panel opens.

③ Click a set in which to create your action.

Photoshop starts with a single set called Default Actions.

● You can click ▣ to create a new actions set.

④ Click the **Create New Action** button (▣) to open the New Action dialog box.

⑤ Type a name for your action.

⑥ Click **Record**.

⑦ Perform the sequence of commands that you want to automate on your images.

● In this example, the first command, Auto Contrast, is performed by clicking **Image** and then **Auto Contrast**.

When automatically optimizing contrast, Photoshop performs a Levels adjustment.

Note: See Chapter 7 for more about adjusting colors and contrast.

● In this example, the second command is performed by clicking **Image**, **Adjustments**, and then **Desaturate**. It converts the image to black and white.

⑧ Click the **Stop** button (■) to stop recording.

● The Actions panel lists the commands performed under the name of the action.

What if I make a mistake when recording my action?

You can try recording the action again by clicking ▾≡ in the Actions panel and clicking **Record Again**. This runs through the same actions, and you can apply different settings in the command dialog boxes. Alternatively, you can select the action, click the **Trash** icon (🗑) to delete the action, and try rerecording it.

How can I control how fast the steps of an action are performed?

In the Actions panel, click ▾≡ and then **Playback Options**. A dialog box appears, enabling you to insert a pause after each step of an action. This can help you review the changes Photoshop makes to an image as it performs an action. The default behavior in Photoshop is to complete the actions as quickly as possible.

Play an Action

You can play an action from the Actions panel on an image. This saves time because you can execute multiple Photoshop commands with a single click. You can also play a specific command that is part of an action by itself.

Play an Action

PLAY A FULL ACTION

1 Click **Window**.

2 Click **Actions**.

The Actions panel opens.

3 Click ▷ (▷ changes to ▽) to open an actions folder.

Photoshop comes with several predefined actions in the Default Actions folder.

Note: To create your own action, see the section "Record an Action."

4 Click the action that you want to play.

5 Click the **Play Selection** button (▶).

Photoshop applies the action's commands to the image.

In this example, a sepia tone is applied to the image.

You can undo the multiple commands in an action using the History panel.

Note: See Chapter 2 for more information about the History panel.

PLAY A COMMAND IN AN ACTION

1 In the Actions panel, click ▷ to reveal the commands that make up an action (▷ changes to ▽).

2 Click the command that you want to execute.

You can Shift +click to select multiple sequential commands.

3 Ctrl +click ▶ (⌘ +click ▶ on a Mac).

Photoshop executes the selected command, but not the commands before or after it.

In this example, the selected command adds noise to the image.

Note: *To execute a specific command and all those after it in an action, select the command and click ▶ without pressing* Ctrl *(* ⌘ *).*

How do I assign a special key command to an action?

1 Click ▼≡ to open the Actions panel menu.

2 Click **Action Options**.

3 In the Action Options dialog box, click ▾ and select a key command.

4 Click **OK**.

To perform an action on an image, press the key selected in Step 3.

Note: *You may want to avoid assigning function keys that are already associated with a command. To view assigned key commands, click* **Edit** *and then* **Keyboard Shortcuts**.

Batch Process by Using an Action

You can apply an action to multiple images automatically with Photoshop's Batch command. The command is a great timesaver for tasks such as optimizing or resizing large numbers of digital photos.

Batch Process by Using an Action

1. Place all the images you want to apply an action to in a source folder.

2. Create a destination folder in which to save your batch-processed files.

Note: To work with folders, see your operating system's documentation.

3. In Photoshop, click **File**.

4. Click **Automate**.

5. Click **Batch**.

The Batch dialog box appears.

6. Click here and select an action to apply.

7. Click **Choose**.

The Browse For Folder (Choose a batch folder on a Mac) dialog box appears.

8. In Windows, click ▷ to open folders on your computer (▷ changes to ◢).

On a Mac, navigate to your source folder.

9. Click the folder containing your images.

10. Click **OK** (click **Choose** on a Mac).

⑪ Click here and select **Folder**.

⑫ Click **Choose** and repeat Steps **8** to **10** to select the folder where you want your batch-processed files to be saved.

● You can specify a naming scheme for saving the batch-processed files.

⑬ Click **OK** (click **Choose** on a Mac).

● Photoshop opens each image in the specified folder one at a time and applies the action.

If the action includes a save step, Photoshop automatically saves each image in the destination directory.

● If the action does not include a save step, Photoshop prompts you with a Save As dialog box for each image.

TIPS

How can I change the mode — such as RGB Color or Grayscale — of an image during a batch process depending on its current mode?

When you record the original action, click **File**, **Automate**, and then **Conditional Mode Change**. A dialog box appears and asks you to specify the source modes that you want to switch as well as a target mode. When the action is run as a batch process, images that are of a selected source mode are converted.

How do I batch process using an action in Mac OS X?

You do this very much like a Windows user does, but with the Open dialog box instead of the Browse for Folder dialog box. When you click **Choose** in Step **7**, the Open-style dialog box appears. Using the file browser in the center of the dialog box, locate the source and destination folders for your batch-processed images.

Create a PDF of Images

Photoshop can automatically create a PDF (Portable Document Format) file that shows one or more of your photos. You can choose from a number of PDF templates, including ones for contact sheets and greeting cards.

You can view PDF files on your computer using the free Adobe Acrobat Reader. Download it here: www.adobe.com/acrobat. On a Mac, you can also use the Preview application.

Create a PDF of Images

1 Open Adobe Bridge by clicking **Launch Bridge** (🔳) in Photoshop.

Note: For more about accessing Bridge, see Chapter 1.

2 Click **Window**.

3 Click **Workspace**.

4 Click **Output**.

Bridge displays panes for outputting images.

5 Make sure the **PDF** button is selected.

6 Click the **Folders** tab.

7 Click ▶ to open folders on your computer (▶ changes to ▼).

8 Click the folder containing your images.

The folder images appear in the bottom pane.

9 Ctrl +click (⌘ +click on a Mac) to select the images you want to save in your PDF.

You can press Ctrl + A (⌘ + A on a Mac) to select all the images in the folder.

10 Click here and select a PDF template.

11 Click **Refresh Preview**.

● Bridge displays a preview of the PDF.

12 Click here to scroll down to the bottom of the Output pane.

13 Click **Save**.

The Save dialog box appears.

14 Click here to select where to save your PDF file.

15 Type a name for your PDF file.

16 Click **Save**.

Bridge saves your PDF and displays a confirmation dialog box.

17 Click **OK**.

What are the different customization options for PDF files in the Output pane?

● **Document Options**: Allow you to choose the paper size and orientation. You can also password-protect your file.

● **Layout Options**: Allow you to change the organization and spacing of the images on the page.

● **Overlays Options**: Allow you to display file name information over your images.

● **Playback Options**: Allow you to control how your PDF appears when viewed as a slideshow.

● **Watermark Options**: Allow you to place transparent text over your images to indicate ownership or other information.

Create a Web Photo Gallery

You can have Photoshop create a photo gallery Web site that showcases your images. Photoshop not only sizes and optimizes your image files for the gallery, but also creates the Web pages that display the images and builds the links and buttons that let you navigate the pages.

BUILD AND PREVIEW A GALLERY

1. Place the images that you want to put into a gallery in a folder.

2. Open Adobe Bridge by clicking **Launch Bridge** (Br icon) in Photoshop.

Note: For more about accessing Bridge, see Chapter 1.

3. Click **Window**.

4. Click **Workspace**.

5. Click **Output**.

   Bridge displays panes for outputting images.

6. Click **Web Gallery**.

7. Click the **Folders** tab.

8. Click (▶ icon) to open folders on your computer (▶ changes to ▼).

9. Click the folder containing your images.

The folder images appear in the bottom pane.

⑩ Ctrl+click (⌘+click on a Mac) to select the images you want to display in your gallery.

You can press Ctrl+A (⌘+A on a Mac) to select all the images in the folder.

⑪ Click here and select a gallery template.

⑫ Click here and select a gallery style for your template. The styles may vary depending on the template chosen.

⑬ Type a gallery title. In most templates, this appears at the top of your gallery pages.

⑭ Type a caption and other descriptive information for your gallery.

⑮ You can type your name and e-mail address if you want people to be able to contact you through your gallery.

How can I customize the colors or layout of my photo gallery?

Under the Color Palette section of the Output pane you can click color swatches to customize the colors of text, background, and other elements in your gallery. In the Appearance section, you can select the number of columns and rows, and choose the preview size of the gallery images.

Do all the photo galleries require Adobe Flash?

Most of the Photoshop gallery templates make use of Adobe Flash to add interactive features such as animated buttons and transitions between images. Viewers must have Flash installed in their Web browsers to view your photos. You can select the HTML Gallery template in Step **10** to create a gallery based only on HTML, which means users do not need to have Flash installed to view it.

continued

After you create your gallery, you can preview it in Bridge or a Web browser. Then you can save it to your computer or upload it to a Web server using Photoshop's integrated FTP client.

To upload your files to a Web server, you will need an Internet connection.

Create a Web Photo Gallery *(continued)*

16 Click **Refresh Preview**.

● Photoshop displays a preview of the gallery.

● You can click links or thumbnail images in the preview to view larger-sized images.

● You can click **Preview in Browser** to view the gallery in your computer's default Web browser.

SAVE TO YOUR COMPUTER

1 Click here to scroll to the bottom of the Output pane.

2 Type a gallery name. Photoshop stores the files in a folder with that name.

3 Click **Save to Disk** (○ changes to ◉).

4 Click **Browse**.

The Choose a Folder dialog box appears.

5 Click to select a location in which to save your gallery.

6 Click **OK** (click **Choose** on a Mac).

7 Click **Save**.

● Photoshop saves the gallery in the specified location and displays a confirmation dialog box.

You can view the saved gallery on your computer by opening the gallery folder and opening the index.html file in a Web browser.

UPLOAD TO THE WEB

1 Type a gallery name. Photoshop uploads the files to a folder with that name.

2 Click **Upload** (○ changes to ●).

3 Type the login information for the FTP server. You can check with your Internet service provider for this information.

4 To upload your gallery to a specific folder, type the folder name here.

5 Click **Upload**.

Photoshop uploads the gallery files.

 TIPS

How can I save my FTP settings?

After you type your user name, password, and other settings in the Upload section, you can save the settings as a preset by clicking 🔲. The New Preset window opens and you can name your preset. Your saved presets can be selected from the menu in the Upload section. To delete a saved preset, select it from the menu and click 🗑.

How can I change the behavior of the panels in the Output pane?

You can click **Edit** (**Adobe Bridge CS4** on a Mac) and then **Preferences** to open the preferences dialog box. Then you can click **Output** to choose your options. If you select the **Use Solo Mode for Output Panel Behavior** option (changes to ✓), only one of the secondary panels in the Output pane will be active at a time. This is convenient if you would rather click headings to access the output options instead of scrolling.

Create a Panoramic Image

You can use the Photomerge feature in Photoshop to stitch several images together into a single panoramic image. This enables you to capture more scenery than is usually possible in a regular photograph.

Create a Panoramic Image

① Click **File**.

② Click **Automate**.

③ Click **Photomerge**.

The Photomerge dialog box appears.

④ Click **Auto** (◎ changes to ◉).

With the Auto setting, Photoshop automatically chooses the best method for stitching your photos together.

⑤ Click **Browse**.

The Open dialog box appears.

⑥ Click here and select the folder that contains the images you want to merge.

⑦ Ctrl +click (⌘+click on a Mac) the images you want to merge into a panoramic image.

⑧ Click **OK**.

● The file names of the images appear in the Source Files list.

9 Click **OK** to build the panoramic image.

Photoshop merges the images into a single panoramic image.

● Parts of each image appear in separate layers in the Layers panel.

Note: For more about layers, see Chapter 8.

● You can use the Crop tool () to remove extra space around the panorama.

Note: For more about cropping, see Chapter 3.

10 Click **File** and then **Save** to save the panorama.

TIP

How can I create photos that merge successfully?
To merge photos successfully, you need to align and overlap the photos as you shoot them. Here are a few hints:

● Use a tripod to keep your photos level with one another.

● Experiment with the different layout modes in the Photomerge dialog box.

● Refrain from using lenses, such as fisheye lenses, that distort your photos.

● Shoot your photos so they overlap at between 30 to 50 percent.

Convert File Types

You can quickly and easily convert images from one file type to another in Photoshop using the Image Processor script. This makes it easy to convert a collection of TIFF files to the JPEG format for posting on the Web.

The Image Processor script allows you to convert to the JPEG, PSD, and TIFF file formats only.

Convert File Types

① Place the images that you want to convert in a folder.

Note: To work with folders, see your operating system's documentation.

② Click **File**.

③ Click **Scripts**.

④ Click **Image Processor**.

The Image Processor dialog box appears.

⑤ Click **Select Folder**.

The Choose Folder (Choose a folder on a Mac) dialog box appears.

⑥ In Windows, click ▷ to open folders on your computer (▷ changes to ◢).

On a Mac, navigate to your source folder

⑦ Click the folder containing your images.

⑧ Click **OK**.

9 Specify where you want your processed images to be saved.

10 Select an image file type option (□ changes to ☑).

● If you select **JPEG**, you can also specify a quality setting from 1 to 12; the higher the quality setting, the larger the resulting file size.

You can select multiple format check boxes; Photoshop saves a separate image file for each format selected.

● You can optionally select **Resize to Fit** (□ changes to ☑), type a new width and height, and Photoshop resizes the images before saving.

Note: *Photoshop leaves the proportions of any resized images unchanged.*

● You can optionally select **Run Action** (□ changes to ☑) to have an action executed on each image before saving.

Note: *For more on actions, see the other tasks in this chapter.*

11 Click **Run**.

Photoshop processes the images.

TIPS

How can I quickly add the same copyright information to multiple images?

In the Image Processor dialog box, type the copyright information into the Copyright Info field. Photoshop adds the information to the processed images. To view the copyright information of an image in Photoshop, open the image and click **File** and then **File Info**.

How can I save my Image Processor settings so I can use them again later?

Click **Save** in the Image Processor dialog box. Another dialog box appears, enabling you to save the settings as an XML file. To load previously saved settings, click **Load** in the Image Processor dialog box.

Batch Rename Images

You can change the file names of multiple images automatically with Bridge's renaming feature. You can customize the new name using custom text, the date, sequential numbers, and more.

Batch Rename Images

1. Place the images that you want to rename in a folder.

2. Open Adobe Bridge by clicking **Launch Bridge** (🗺) in Photoshop.

Note: For more about accessing Bridge, see Chapter 1.

3. Click the **Folders** tab.

4. Click the folder containing the images to rename.

5. Click **Tools**.

6. Click **Batch Rename**.

The Batch Rename dialog box opens.

● By default, the renamed images are saved in the same folder.

● You can click the **Move** or **Copy** options to save the images elsewhere. After you click Move or Copy, you can click **Browse** to select a destination folder.

⑦ Click here and select a file naming option.

⑧ Type in text boxes or select from menus to customize the file name.

In this example, the images are renamed with a capitalized version of their file name.

⑨ Repeat Steps **7** and **8** for other parts of the naming scheme.

● You can add or remove naming scheme options by clicking ⊞ or ⊟, respectively.

● An example of the new file name appears.

⑩ Click **Rename**.

Photoshop renames the images in the folder.

How can I rename images based on the camera settings they were taken with?

Select **Metadata** for a file name option in Step **7** and then select a camera setting in the menu that appears. You can use aperture value, exposure setting, focal length, and other camera settings in your new file names.

How can I save my renaming settings for use later?

Click **Save** in the Batch Rename dialog box. A Save As dialog box appears, enabling you to save the settings. To load previously saved settings, click **Load** in the Batch Rename dialog box.

Using Tool Presets

You can specify commonly used options for a tool and then save that set of options for later use. For example, it can be helpful to define presets for brush styles and opacities you use often.

Using Tool Presets

DEFINE A TOOL PRESET

1 Click a tool.

2 In the options bar, specify the settings you want to save for that tool.

3 Click ▾.

● Previously defined and default presets are listed.

4 Click the **Create New Tool Preset** button (📄).

5 In the New Tool Preset dialog box, type a name for the tool preset.

6 Click **OK**.

Photoshop saves the tool preset.

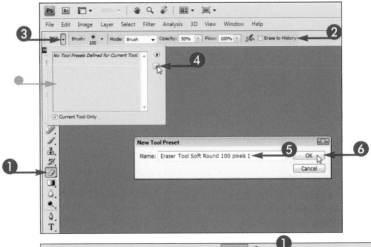

LOAD A TOOL PRESET

1 Click **Window**.

2 Click **Tool Presets**.

The Tool Presets panel opens, listing the presets available for that tool.

● You can deselect **Current Tool Only** (✓ changes to ▢) to display the presets for all the tools.

③ Click a preset.

● The tool settings in the options bar change to reflect those defined in the preset.

④ You can apply the tool to see the effects of the preset.

How can I easily manage a large number of tool presets?

The Tool Presets panel menu features a variety of commands for managing your presets.

① Click 📋 to open the Tool Presets panel menu.

② Click a command.

● You can open the Preset Manager to view and organize your presets in a dialog box. You can also access it by clicking **Edit** and then **Preset Manager**.

● You can save groups of presets as separate files on your computer and then reload them later.

Saving and Printing Images

You can save your images for use later, or so that you can use them in another application or on the Web. You can also print out your images to have a hard copy of your work. This chapter shows you how.

Save in the Photoshop Format

You can save your image in Photoshop's native image format. This format enables you to retain multiple layers in your image, if it has them. This is the best format in which to save your images if you still need to edit them.

Photoshop PDF and TIFF files also support multiple layers.

Save in the Photoshop Format

① Click **File**.

② Click **Save As**.

● If you have named and saved your image previously and just want to save changes, you can click **File** and then **Save**.

The Save As dialog box appears.

③ Click here and then click a folder in which to save the image file.

④ Click here and select the Photoshop file format.

⑤ Type a name for the image file.

Photoshop automatically assigns a .psd extension if you do not specify an extension.

- To save a copy of the file and keep the existing file open, you can select **As a Copy** (☐ changes to ☑).

- To merge the multiple layers of your image into one layer, you can deselect **Layers** (☑ changes to ☐).

6 Click **Save**.

The Photoshop Format Options dialog box appears.

7 Click **OK** to make sure your image is compatible with other applications.

Photoshop saves the image file.

- The name of the file appears in the image's title bar.

 TIP

What are the shortcuts for saving an image in Photoshop?
You can use several keyboard commands to save your image:

Command	Windows Shortcut	Mac Shortcut
Save	Ctrl + S	⌘ + S
Save As	Shift + Ctrl + S	Shift + ⌘ + S
Save for Web & Devices	Alt + Shift + Ctrl + S	Option + Shift + ⌘ + S

Save an Image for Use in Another Application

You can save your image in a format that can be opened and used in other imaging or page layout applications. TIFF (Tagged Image File Format) and EPS (Encapsulated PostScript) are standard printing formats that many applications on both Windows and Mac platforms support.

BMP – bitmap – is a popular Windows image format, and PICT is a Macintosh image format.

Note that most image formats – with the exception of Photoshop PSD, Photoshop PDF, Large Document, and TIFF – do not support layers.

Save an Image for Use in Another Application

1 Click **File**.

2 Click **Save As**.

The Save As dialog box appears.

3 Click here and select a folder in which to save the image file.

4 Click here and select a file format.

If you are saving a multilayer image and you select a file format that does not support layers, an alert icon appears. Photoshop saves a flattened copy of the image.

Note: *See the section "Save in the Photoshop Format" to save a multilayer image. For more about flattening, see Chapter 8.*

5 Type a file name.

Photoshop automatically assigns an appropriate extension for the file format, such as .tif for TIFF or .eps for EPS, if you do not specify an extension.

6 Click **Save**.

A dialog box appears with options specific to the format in which you are saving — the TIFF format, in this example.

7 Click **OK**.

Photoshop saves the image.

If a flattened copy is saved, the original multilayer version remains in the image window.

TIPS

How do I choose a file format for my image?

You should choose the format based on how you want to use the image. If it is a multilayered image and you want to preserve the layers, save it as a Photoshop file or TIFF. If you want to use the image in word processing or page layout applications, save it as a TIFF or EPS file. If you want to use the image on the Web, save it as a JPEG, PNG, or GIF file. For more information on file formats, see the rest of this chapter as well as Photoshop's documentation.

How can I save several images as a presentation?

You can click **File**, **Automate**, and then **PDF Presentation** to save images as a slideshow presentation. The PDF Presentation dialog box appears, enabling you to select your slideshow images, a background, and the duration between slides. After you save the presentation, you can view it in Adobe Reader, which can be downloaded free from www.adobe.com. Mac users can also use the Preview application.

Save a JPEG for the Web

You can save a file in the JPEG — Joint Photographic Experts Group — format and publish it on the Web. JPEG is the most common file format for saving photographic images.

Photoshop saves JPEG images at 72 dpi.

① Click **File**.

② Click **Save for Web & Devices**.

The Save for Web & Devices dialog box appears.

③ Click the **2-Up** tab.

④ Click here to select the optimized version of your image.

⑤ Click here and select **JPEG**.

⑥ Click here and select a quality setting.

● Alternatively, you can select a numeric quality setting from 0 (low quality) to 100 (high quality).

The higher the quality, the larger the resulting file size.

⑦ Check that the file quality and size are acceptable in the preview pane.

● You can use the **Hand** tool (🖐) to move the image in the preview window.

● You can use the **Zoom** tool (🔍) to magnify the image in the preview window.

⑧ Click **Save**.

⑨ In Windows, click here and select a folder in which to save the file.

On a Mac, use the Where pop-up menu or the File Browser to select a folder.

⑩ Type a file name. Photoshop automatically assigns a .jpg extension if you do not include an extension.

⑪ Click **Save**.

The original image file remains open in Photoshop.

TIPS

What is image compression?

Image compression involves using mathematical techniques to reduce the amount of information required to describe an image. This results in smaller file sizes, which is important when transmitting information on the Web. Some compression schemes, such as JPEG, reduce image quality somewhat, but the loss is usually negligible compared to the savings in file size.

How can I optimize my Web images to a specific file size?

In the Save for Web & Devices dialog box, click ≡ in the upper right corner and select **Optimize to File Size**. A dialog box appears, allowing you to specify a target file size and other settings. Click **OK** to have Photoshop automatically select optimization settings to meet your requirements. The tool works with regular images and sliced images. For more about saving sliced images, see "Save a Sliced Image."

Save a GIF for the Web

You can save an image as a GIF — Graphics Interchange Format — file and publish it on the Web. The GIF format is good for saving illustrations that have a limited number of colors. The format supports a maximum of 256 colors.

Photoshop saves GIF images at 72 dpi. Unlike JPEG images, GIF images can include transparency.

① Click **File**.

② Click **Save for Web & Devices**.

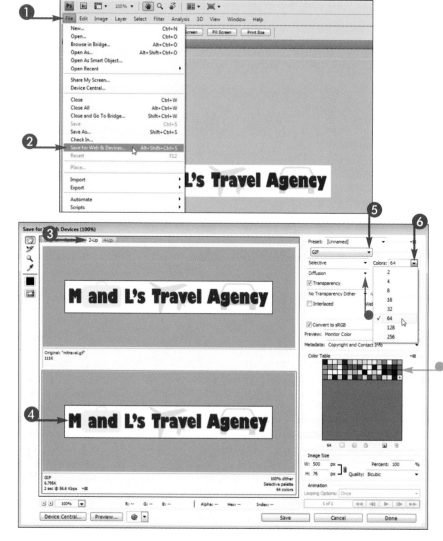

The Save for Web & Devices dialog box appears.

③ Click the **2-Up** tab.

④ Click here to select the optimized version of your image.

⑤ Click here and select GIF.

⑥ Click here and select the number of colors to include in the image.

● The Color Table displays the included colors.

GIF allows a maximum of 256 colors.

● You can click here to choose the algorithm Photoshop uses to select the GIF colors.

7 Check that the file quality and size are acceptable in the preview window.

● You can use 🖑 to move the image in the preview pane.

● You can use 🔍 to magnify the image in the preview pane.

● Selecting **Transparency** (🔲 changes to ☑) ensures that any transparent areas of your image remain that way in your final GIF image.

8 Click **Save**.

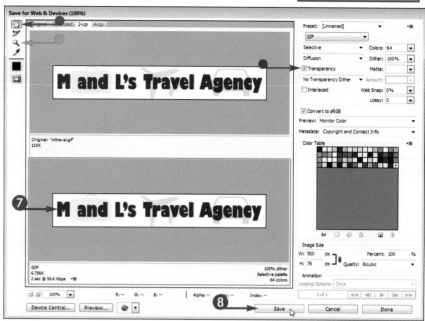

9 In Windows, click here and select a folder in which to save the file.

On a Mac, use the Where pop-up menu or the File Browser to select a folder.

10 Type a file name. Photoshop automatically assigns a .gif extension if you do not add an extension.

11 Click **Save**.

The original image file remains open in Photoshop.

TIPS

How do I minimize the file sizes of my GIF images?

The most important factor in creating small GIFs is limiting the number of colors in the final image. GIF files are limited to 256 colors or fewer. In images that have just a few solid colors, you can often reduce the total number of colors to 16 or even 8 without any noticeable reduction in quality. See Step 6 in this section to set the number of colors in your GIF images.

How can I use GIF transparency in my Web images?

GIF images that include transparency allow the background of a Web page to show through. Transparent GIFs enable you to add nonrectangular elements into your Web projects. Because Background layers cannot contain transparent pixels, you need to work with layers other than the Background layer to create transparent GIFs. See Chapter 8 for more about layers.

Save a PNG for the Web

You can save an image as a PNG — Portable Network Graphics — file and publish it on the Web.

PNG was devised as a higher-quality alternative to GIF. Unlike GIF, PNG can support more than 256 colors. However, it is not as universally supported as GIF and JPEG are by older Web browsers.

Save a PNG for the Web

1 Click **File**.

2 Click **Save for Web & Devices**.

The Save for Web & Devices dialog box appears.

3 Click the **2-Up** tab.

4 Click here to select the optimized version of your image.

5 Click here and select **PNG-8** or **PNG-24**.

Note: See the tip on the opposite page for details about the different PNG settings.

6 Check that the file quality and size are acceptable in the preview pane.

● You can use to move the image in the preview pane.

● You can use 🔍 to magnify the image in the preview pane.

● Selecting **Transparency** (☐ changes to ☑) ensures that any transparent areas of your image remain that way in your final PNG image.

7 Click **Save**.

8 In Windows, click here and select a folder in which to save the file.

On a Mac, use the Where pop-up menu or the File Browser to select a folder.

9 Type a file name. Photoshop automatically assigns a .png extension if you do not add an extension.

10 Click **Save**.

The original image file remains open in Photoshop.

TIPS

What is the difference between the PNG-8 and PNG-24 settings?

PNG-8 stands for PNG 8-bit. With it, you can limit the number of colors in the final PNG image and thereby decrease the resulting file size. PNG-24 stands for PNG 24-bit. This format includes a wider range of colors than 8-bit and leads to better image quality, but generally results in much larger file sizes.

How does the PNG format support transparency?

Like GIF files, PNG files can include transparency. But unlike GIFs, the PNG format supports a more advanced feature called alpha-channel transparency, which allows a background behind an image to show through partially. You can add partial transparency to your image by decreasing the opacity of a layer. For more information about layers and opacity, see Chapter 8.

Add Descriptive and Copyright Information

You can store title, author, description, and copyright information with your saved image. You may find this useful if you plan on publishing the images online and want them to retain information about their source.

Some image-editing applications — such as Photoshop — can detect copyright information in an image and display it when the image is opened.

Add Descriptive and Copyright Information

1 Click **File**.

2 Click **File Info**.

The File Info dialog box appears.

3 Type title and author information for the image.

4 Type a description for the image.

5 Type keywords for the image.

⑥ Click here and select a copyright status.

⑦ Type the copyright information for the image.

⑧ Click **OK**.

● If you mark the image as copyrighted, Photoshop places a copyright symbol in the title bar.

To save the image, see the other tasks in this chapter.

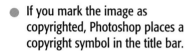

How do I view information about a photo taken with a digital camera?

You can access information about photos taken with a digital camera in the File Info dialog box. You can view the information by clicking the **Camera Data** tab in the dialog box. The information includes the model of the camera, date and time the photo was shot, shutter speed, aperture value, and more.

What is a Creative Commons copyright license?

The File Info dialog box allows you to apply one of several licenses from the Creative Commons, abbreviated CC, to your images. Creative Commons licenses are useful when you want to allow public use of your images but with certain restrictions. Restrictions might include only noncommercial use or attribution of the original owner. For more information, visit www.creativecommons.org.

Save a Sliced Image

You can save an image that has been partitioned with the Slice tool. Photoshop saves the slices as separate images and also saves an HTML file that organizes the slices into a Web page. Slices enable you to save different parts of an image as JPEGs, GIFs, or PNGs. This can result in a smaller overall file size for the image.

For more information about using the Slice tool, see Chapter 4.

Save a Sliced Image

① Open your sliced image.

② Click **File**.

③ Click **Save for Web & Devices**.

The Save for Web & Devices dialog box appears.

④ Click **Optimized**.

⑤ Click the **Slice Select** tool (✐).

⑥ Click one of the image slices to select it.

⑦ Specify the optimization settings for the slice.

⑧ Repeat Steps **6** and **7** for each of the slices.

⑨ Click **Save**.

⑩ In Windows, click here and select a folder in which to save the file.

On a Mac, use the Where pop-up menu or the File Browser to select a folder.

⑪ In Windows, click here and select **HTML and Images** as the file type.

On a Mac, click the **Format** ⬦ and select **HTML and Images**.

⑫ Type the name of the HTML file that will organize the slices.

Photoshop saves the images by appending slice numbers to the original image name.

● To change the naming scheme, you can click here and select **Other**.

⑬ Click **Save**.

You can access the HTML and image files in the folder that you specified in Step **10**.

● The image files are saved in a separate images subfolder.

● To view the Web page, you can double-click the HTML file. The file opens in a Web browser.

How do I publish my Web page online?

After you create a Web page by saving your sliced Photoshop image, you can make the page available online by transferring the HTML and image files to a Web server using an FTP program. Most people arrange for Web server access through an Internet service provider, or ISP. Mac OS X users also have the Apache Web server built into their computer's operating system.

How do I preview my optimized image in a Web browser from inside Photoshop?

You can click **Preview** at the bottom of the Save for Web & Devices dialog box to open your optimized image in your computer's default Web browser. Photoshop also lists statistics for the image, including the format, dimensions, and file size, in the browser window. After you preview the image in the browser, you can switch back to Photoshop to change the optimization settings or save the image.

Print on a PC

You can print your Photoshop image on a PC using an inkjet, laser, or other type of printer.

You can preview your printout – as well as adjust the size and positioning of your printed image – before printing.

Print on a PC

1 Make sure the layers you want to print are visible.

Note: *The visibility icon (👁) means that a layer is visible. For more about layers, see Chapter 8.*

2 Click **File**.

3 Click **Print**.

● To quickly print a single copy without previewing, you can click **Print One Copy**.

The Print dialog box appears.

4 Type a percentage in the Scale box to shrink or enlarge the image.

5 To resize the image by dragging the corners, select the **Bounding Box** option (▢ changes to ☑).

6 Deselect **Center Image** to allow repositioning of the image (☑ changes to ▢).

306

⑦ Click and drag in the image window to reposition the image on the page.

● You can position your image precisely by typing values in the Top and Left fields.

● You can click and drag the handles on the image corners to scale the image by hand.

⑧ Click ⟨-⟩ and choose a printer.

⑨ Type the number of copies to print.

⑩ Click **Print**.

A smaller Print dialog box appears.

● You can click **Preferences** to set printer-specific options.

⑪ Click **Print** to print the image.

TIPS

How can I maximize the size of my image on the printed page?
In the Print Preview dialog box, you can select the **Scale to Fit Media** option (☐ changes to ☑) to scale the image to the maximum size given the current print settings.

How can I print just a selected part of an image?
Before performing the Print with Preview, select a part of your image with the Rectangular Marquee tool (▱). Select the **Print Selected Area** option (☐ changes to ☑) in the Print dialog box. This feature does not work with areas selected using the Elliptical Marquee, Lasso, or Magic Wand tools.

You can print your Photoshop image in color or black and white on a Mac using an inkjet, laser, or other type of printer.

① Make sure the layers you want to print are visible.

Note: The visibility icon (👁) means that a layer is visible. For more about layers, see Chapter 8.

② Click **File**.

③ Click **Print**.

● To quickly print a single copy without previewing, you can click **Print One Copy**.

The Print dialog box appears.

④ Type a percentage in the Scale box to shrink or enlarge the image.

⑤ To resize the image, select the **Bounding Box** option (☐ changes to ☑).

⑥ Deselect **Center Image** to allow repositioning of the image (☑ changes to ☐).

7 Click and drag in the image window to reposition the image on the page.

● You can position your image precisely by typing values in the Top and Left fields.

● You can click and drag the handles on the image corners to scale the image by hand.

8 Click ▣ and choose a printer.

9 Type the number of copies to print.

10 Click **Print**.

A smaller Print dialog box appears.

● You can set the number of copies to print in the **Copies** text box.

● You can set printer-specific options from the pop-up menu categories that appear.

Note: See the tip on re-creating a group of printer settings to make future print session setups fast and easy.

11 Click **Print** to print the image.

What is halftoning?

In grayscale printing, *halftoning* is the process by which a printer creates the appearance of different shades of gray using only black ink. If you look closely at a grayscale image printed on most black-and-white laser printers, you see that the image consists of tiny, differently sized dots. Larger dots produce the darker gray areas of the image, and smaller dots produce the lighter gray areas.

How do I save a group of printer settings on a Mac?

After specifying the settings for a print job, click the **Presets** pop-up menu, choose **Save As**, and give the settings a name. You can access your saved printer settings in the Presets pop-up menu in the Print dialog box.

Index

Index

formatting type, 260–261
frame borders, layers, 7
Freeform Pen tool, 251
FTP settings, 281
full screen mode, 38

G

galleries
    color customizing, 279
    Flash, 279
Gaussian Blur dialog box, 218
ghosted white covering, 119
GIF files
    saving for Web, 298–299
    size, 299
    transparency, 299
Glowing Edges filter, 230–231
gradient, color gradient on type, 263
Gradient Editor, 114
Gradient tool, 31
gradients
    applying, 114–115
    customizing, 115
    linear, 114
grayscale
    duotones and, 160
    halftoning, 309
grouping images, Bridge, 25
guides
    moving, 41
    snapping to, 41

H

halftoning, 309
Hand tool
    description, 31
    views and, 36–37
Healing Brush tool, 126–127
Help, 16–17
hidden tools
    description, 31
    selecting, 32
hiding, layers, 172
highlights, correcting, 158–159

History Brush tool
    Art History Brush, 131
    description, 30
    painting previous state, 130–131
History panel, number of operations saved, 13
horizontal lines, drawing, 249
hue, adjusting, 148–149
Hue/Saturation dialog box, 148–149

I

image compression, 297
Image Processor dialog box, 284–285
Image Size dialog box, 48–49
image windows, 10, 44–45
images
    browsing for, 20–21
    canvas size, 58–59
    copyright information, 302–303
    creating, 26
    cropping, 54–56
    descriptives, 302–303
    filtering in Bridge, 23
    folders (Bridge), 21
    grouping in Bridge, 25
    labels, 21
    layers, copying between, 171
    new, 11
    offsetting, 234–235
    on-screen sizing, 48–49
    opening, 18–19
    optimizing, 297
    overexposed, 165
    panoramic, 282–283
    print size, 50–51, 307
    printing on Mac, 308–309
    printing on PC, 306–307
    ratings, 21
    renaming, 286–287
    resolution, 52–53
    reverting to previously saved, 43
    saving as copies, 293
    saving as presentation, 295
    saving for use in another application, 294–295
    saving for Web, 49

Index

Index

Index

Vibrance command, 164–165
Vibrance dialog box, 164–165
viewing information about images, 303
views
    Hand tool and, 36
    scroll bars, 37
virtual slider, 109

W

Warp Text dialog box, 266–267
warp type, 266–267
Web
    saving GIF files to, 298–299
    saving JPEG files for, 296–297
    saving PNG files to, 300–301
Web Gallery
    colors, customizing, 279
    creating, 278–279

save to computer, 280–281
    uploading to Web, 281
Web pages, publishing, 305
Web-safe colors, 105
windows
    copying selections between, 87
    image windows, 44–45
    tabbed, 45
workspaces, saving, 14–15

Z

Zoom tool
    description, 31
    magnifying and, 34–35

Read Less–Learn More®

Visual®

There's a Visual book
for every learning level...

Simplified®

The place to start if you're new to computers. Full color.

- Computers
- Creating Web Pages
- Mac OS
- Office
- Windows

Teach Yourself VISUALLY™

Get beginning to intermediate-level training in a variety of topics. Full color.

- Access
- Bridge
- Chess
- Computers
- Crocheting
- Digital Photography
- Dog training
- Dreamweaver
- Excel
- Flash
- Golf
- Guitar
- Handspinning
- HTML
- Jewelry Making & Beading
- Knitting
- Mac OS
- Office
- Photoshop
- Photoshop Elements
- Piano
- Poker
- PowerPoint
- Quilting
- Scrapbooking
- Sewing
- Windows
- Wireless Networking
- Word

Top 100 Simplified® Tips & Tricks

Tips and techniques to take your skills beyond the basics. Full color.

- Digital Photography
- eBay
- Excel
- Google
- Internet
- Mac OS
- Office
- Photoshop
- Photoshop Elements
- PowerPoint
- Windows

...all designed for visual learners—just like you!